PLANTATION TOURS & TASTES

Georgetown History and Lowcountry cooking at its best

Garden at Prince George Winyah   Artist: Jean Littler

Published by
The Church Women of Prince George Winyah Parish
Georgetown, South Carolina

ISBN: 978-0-9786827-0-5

Library of Congress Control Number: 2006929240

Copies of PLANTATION TOURS AND TASTES may be obtained by sending $29.95 plus $5.00 shipping and handling to the following address:

Plantation Tours and Tastes
Prince George Winyah Parish
Highmarket and Broad Streets
P.O. Box 674
Georgetown, South Carolina 29442

Are these regional recipes? Certainly! How big is your "Region"? Is it where you were born or where you grew up? Does this book contain recipes from the English who settled here in the 1700's or from the African traditions of the same period? Are there recipes from France around 1719? Recipes from Lebanon and Scotland? Jewish recipes of the immigrants from Europe? Some recipes are Old South, some New South, and some "From Off". That is, the food is all delicious and the cooks are, or were, living here. So the recipes are Prince Georges' to share. Therefore, no claim is made as to the originality of these recipes. They have been tried and enjoyed; sometimes altered, adapted and adopted. Please enjoy.

Cover Art: Bell and Clock Tower
Prince George Winyah Parish
Artist: Ray Ellis

WIMMER
COOKBOOKS

A CONSOLIDATED GRAPHICS COMPANY

800.548.2537   wimmerco.com

With Grateful Thanks From

Co-Editors
Jackie Harris
Doris Pioth

We wish to express our appreciation to the parishioners of Prince George Winyah Parish and to our friends, community and local restaurants who took time to share their recipes with us. We regret that we were unable to publish them all due to similarity or availability of space. We have been as diligent as possible in compiling our information, but if we've forgotten to include your name, please know you have been thanked through prayer.

Recipes
Lee Ann Tiller

Art Committee
Susan Tiller   Cheryl Bellune

Artists
Doris Athey	Ray Ellis	Robert Lumpkin
Janet Baril	Lib Ferdon	Danny McLaughlin
Connie Bull	Dian Hammett	Myrna McMahon
Gertrude Bull	Jean Hanna	Kathy Metts
Lon Calhoun	Honley	Elean Parker
Joseph Cave	Lu Hook	Shirley Rigle
Bruce Chandler	Bernie Horton	Jackie Harris
Marcia Constance	Gail Joley	Susan Tiller
Johnnie Cowan	Pat Latstetter	Nancy VanBuren
Michael Dusenberry	Jean Littler	Greg Watkins

Finance
Lois Dwyer   Angela Tiller

Historians
Martha Allison	Sarah Lumpkin, author of
Elizabeth Asnip	HERITAGE PASSED ON
Muff Boyd	Alberta Quattelbaum, author of
Patricia Doyle	RICE PLANTATIONS

Marketing

Sands Gresham	Angela Geer
Mary Gaulpin	Tori Mackey
Hope Weil	

Photographers

Anne Malerich	Paige Sawyer

Typists and Proofreaders

Olga Abbott	Mary Gaulipin
Martha Allison	Sands Gresham
Elizabeth Asnip	Laura Meyer
Emily Aspel	Cathy McCray
Joyce Bourne	Lee McIntyre
Muff Boyd	Kay Mower
Virginia Dugan	Doris Pioth
Lois Dwyer	Jackie Harris
Becky Fuener	Sarah Steen

Proceeds from the sale of PLANTATION TOURS AND TASTES will be used to the glory of God and the upkeep and operation of our historic church facilities.

Recipes in this book include recipes from the original Prince George Winyah cookbook. These recipes have been designated with a sketch of our clock and bell tower.

Prayers, graces and biblical quotes are designated with a sketch of the Cross and Crown. It symbolizes the suffering and death of Jesus as well as his final victory over sin and death.

CONTRIBUTORS

The cookbook committee would like to thank all the parishioners, friends, and restaurants that took the time to share their recipes with us. Without you this book could not have been published. We regret that we were unable to publish all recipes due to similarity or availability of space. We have been as diligent as possible in compiling this list, but if we've forgotten to name you, you have been thanked through prayer.

Olga Abbott
Ernest Abbott
Rita Ahearn
Jennifer Aiken
Martha Allison
Roz Ambrose
Elizabeth Asnip
Thelma Beaubian
Ruth O. Bell
Cheryl Bellune
Lori Bellune
Jody Bennett
Evie Bentz
John Bentz
Joyce Bourne
Carolyn Bowen
Betsy Brabson
Jana Bradley
Sandy Brown
Connie Bull
Emily Bull
Katherine Bull
Gloria Burns
Debbie Butterfield
Eleanor Cambrey
Joan Carraway
Sarah Caughman
Elizabeth Clare
Joy Clark
Faith Coffey
Caroline Crocker
Alice Cromartie
Elise Crosby
Kathy Crosby
Barbie Culbertson
Fran Dawson
Liz Dawson
Lauretta Dean

Renee Dean
Dottie Dixon
Julia Doar
Terry Doar
Amy Downing
Pat Doyle
Karen Dubay
Jennie Dugan
Virginia Dugan
Lois Dwyer
Mary Easley
Joe Ferguson
Pat Ferris
Victoria Fleischer
Lawly Ford
Leila Ford
Liz Forrester
Becky Fuener
Keira Fuener
Mary Galphin
John Gibbs
Mary Jo Gibbs
Wallace Gibbs
Mrs. Frank Graham
Chuck Gresham
Sands Gresham
Norma Grimes
Jane Hallos
Martha Harper
Jackie Harris
Marian Harris
Carlisle Harvard
Miriam Hattori
Alec Hemingway
Dixie Hemingway
Clark Hight
Wallis Houseman
Lisa Hutto
Fran Jackson

Claire Jagger
Carol Jayroe
Page Johnson
Lee Bowen Jones
Nancy Jones
Julia Pyatt Kaminski
Marybeth Kulp
Rebecca Lammonds
Jan Lane
Dana Larson
Michele Lombardi
Sally Lumpkin
Sarah Lumpkin
Anne Lynch
Tory Mackey
Helen Manning
Tricia McCray
Nancy McElveen
Walter McElveen
Patou McIsaac
Lucinda McLean
Darlene McNeil
Laura Meyer
Doug Miller
Gene Miller
Anne Moore
Charlotte Moore
Totsie Moore
Kay Morrow
Kay Mower
Roger Mower
Beth Ness
Stephanie Oxner
Fran Palmer
Sally Parker
Dawn Pate
Boo Peace
Doris Pioth
Vivian Powell

Charles Ragsdale
Emily Ragsdale
Helen Ralston
Gwendolyn Reichow
Madeliene Ritchie
Tom Ritchie
Beth Roberts
Betty Roberts
Tracey Rogers
Wanda Rogers
Joy Sasser
Mary Sasso
Marilyn Sinclair
Bob Siyufy
Julie Stalvey
Pat Stalvey
Anne Starnes
Dave Starnes
Sarah Steen
Laura Stein
Caroline Stevens
Peggy Stockly
Meg Tarbox
Marie Taylor
Brad Tiller
Dorine Tiller
Lee Ann Tiller
Susan Tiller
Natalie Tolino
Bubbie Vereen
Holli Wear
Susan Welch
Emily West
Nancy Wilson
Zella Wilt
Hannah Withers

Restaurant Contributors

Brookgreen Gardens, Murrells Inlet
Café Latte, Calabash
Café Lucia, Pawleys Island
Carefree Catering, Pawleys Island
Chive Blossom Café, Pawleys Island
Drunken Jack's, Murrells Inlet
Franks, Pawleys Island
Harbor House Bed and Breakfast, Georgetown
Independent Seafood, Georgetown
Kudzu Bakery, Georgetown
Litchfield Plantation's Carriage House Club, Pawleys Island
Louis' at Pawleys, Pawleys Island
The Melting Pot, Murrells Inlet
Oliver's Lodge, Murrells Inlet
Orobosa's Lowcountry Café, Pawleys Island
Outback at Frank's, Pawleys Island
The Rice Paddy, Georgetown
Royal Oak Pub, Murrells Inlet
Roz's Rice Mill, Pawleys Island
Sawgrass Room at Pawleys Plantation Golf and Country
Club, Pawleys Island
Southern Market at the Galleria, Myrtle Beach
Thoroughbreds, North Myrtle Beach
Trawlers Restaurant, Mt. Pleasant
Tyler's Cove, Murrells Inlet
Umberto's at Coquina Harbor
Yokoso, North Myrtle Beach

TABLE OF CONTENTS

Prayer of the
Women of the Church

Almighty God, our Heavenly Father, bless we pray Thee, our work for the extension of Thy kingdom, and make us so thankful for the precious gift to us of Thy beloved Son, that we may pray fervently, labor diligently, and give liberally to make Him known to all nations as their Savior and their King, through the same Jesus Christ, our Lord.

Amen.

Prince George Winyah Parish   Artist: Susan Tiller

History

Georgetown, South Carolina occupies a unique place in modern history. In fact, some say that modern history began here in 1526 with the earliest settlement in North America by Europeans, the Spanish under Lucas Vasquez de Allyon on Waccamaw Neck.

Based on the discoveries of Giavanni Caboto, known to the world as John Cabot, Charles I, in 1629, granted to his attorney-general, Sir Robert Heath, a charter to all his majesty's claims, between latitudes 36 and 31, under the name of Carolana. In 1663, Charles II gave a charter for the land, formerly granted to Heath, to eight of his most faithful supporters. These men were known as the Lords Proprietors. The Proprietors could establish the Anglican Church but were also granted the authority to authorize freedom of worship. Any seven or more persons, agreeing in any religion, would qualify as a church or profession to which some name was required in order to distinguish it.

In 1665, Carolina (as it was now called) was divided into three parts: Berkeley, Colleton, and Craven (now known as Georgetown) counties. All three extended inland for thirty-five miles or a day's journey from the Atlantic Ocean. Few white people had settled in Craven County until 1685 when the Huguenots settled on the Santee River to plant rice. They chose a spot to build a church with a town around it which they called Jamestown with seventy families in the original settlement. France's 1685 repeal of religious freedom for non-Catholics sped their arrival. More Huguenots followed and they became one of the colony's greatest assets.

After the settlement of Charles Town in 1670 by the English, trade was established with the Indians, and the trading posts in outlying areas became settlements.

In 1671, over a hundred settlers arrived from Barbados and settled in the Goose Creek area. Although they had been successful planters, they needed more land than was available on that small island. In little time they became strong leaders in the new colony. In Barbados they had established parishes where parochial officers had, not only ecclesiastical, but civil jurisdiction, and this system, as well as the main features of their slave code, was adopted by Carolina.

Although the Anglican Church was not formally established by law in Carolina until 1704, the Assembly in 1698 had marked the course toward making it the established church by passing an act which forbade public support of any church other than that established by law in England. In 1706, a petition was made to the Assembly to divide St. Philip's Parish. The Parish of St. James was formed which included the newly built church at Jamestown. (A parish was an area of land laid out to be committed to the charge of one parson or vicar and under law exercised both civil and ecclesiastical powers.)

As more settlers moved into the northern part of Carolina, the Parish of St. James was divided and the parish of Prince George was established with a wooden church built in 1721 on the Black River on a site about twelve miles from present Georgetown. The church was named for George, Prince of Wales, who later became George II of England

Prince George Parish was divided in 1734. Since the original church fell within the newly established bounds of Prince Frederick Parish, commissioners were appointed to build a new church building for the Prince George Winyah congregation in the growing port of Georgetown. Manufactured goods from Europe, fruit and rum from the West Indies, and bricks

Colonial Anglican churches rarely had stained glass windows but two were installed as memorials in the early 20th century. Some of the original clear panes are still in place in two of the windows on the western side. The church suffered damage from fire in the Revolutionary War and further damage in the Civil War. The original details of adornment have been lost. The chancel was added about 1809 when repairs were made following the Revolution, and the bell tower was added in the 1820's. Prince George is one of the few church buildings in South Carolina which dates back to the colonial period and has served continuously through the years for the faithful in their worship of Almighty God.

and earthenware from New England made Georgetown a bustling port. Rice, pitch, tar, turpentine, skins, sassafras, pork, corn, and peas were exported. In 1731, Georgetown was made an official port of entry with some of the import duties going to help build a church worthy of this growing town. Prominent local families contributed land and various sums of money including the Rev. Thomas Morritt who contributed the communion silver.

Bricks were collected as early as 1740. The Rev. Alexander Keith, the first rector, was sent by the English Society for the Propagation of the Gospel in Foreign Parts. He held the initial service in Prince George Winyah on August 16, 1747 even though some of the furniture was still not in place.

The design of the church was similar to most Anglican churches using the Book of Common

Prayer and contained box pews, pulpit, lectern, and holy table. Charles Woodmason, who later became an Anglican minister, noted in 1766, "This Church is in the Town of Georgetown - is 80 feet by 50 has 3 isles, but no Galleries as yet. The Pulpit and Pews are well executed, but the Altar Piece is not yet up." Pews were sold to raise money to finish the church. Later, pews were rented and then assigned to families but today are open to all. Box pews were the custom in colonial churches. Generations of children entertained themselves surreptitiously by carving on the wood in the pews. One can see sailing ships, a lady with a bustle, the pulpit, and the names, initials, and dates of prior occupants.

Indigo, which was introduced by Eliza Lucas Pinckney in 1740, soon became the cash crop for the settlers. The war of Jenkins Ear (1739-1748) between England and France left England without a source of Royal Blue indigo dye which England used to dye military uniforms among other things. Blue indigo is the rarest of dyes because blue is the most difficult color to produce. Brisk trade in indigo created some large fortunes, but this ended after the Revolutionary War when the English bounty was removed. An aristocratic society was formed with planters owning plantations, and possibly a house in Georgetown and Charleston which they used during the social season. Indigo gave Georgetown County its first source of economic wealth.

Planters, who lived in relative isolation from one another, decided in 1740 to form the Winyah Indigo Society in order to discuss any recent news from London. George II granted the Society a royal charter in 1758. Club members met on the first Friday of each month in Georgetown's Old Oak Tavern. The initiation fee and annual dues were paid in indigo. After it was sold, a large sum of money soon accumulated. In searching for a worthwhile project, they decided to establish an independent charity school for the poor. A hall for the Winyah Indigo Society was later built in 1853 and was used as a meeting place, a school, and a library. During the Civil War, it was also used as a hospital for Federal troops.

During the Revolutionary War, Georgetown played its part by sending Thomas Lynch, Jr., of Hopsewee Plantation, to sign the Declaration of Independence and by receiving the Marquis de Lafayette to our shores from France to help our cause against England. Georgetown became an important port for General Nathaniel Greene's army after Charles Town fell in 1780. Francis Marion led many guerilla actions in the vicinity and earned the name "Swamp Fox."

With the loss of the English subsidy, the planters turned to rice cultivation as their major source of income. Rice required the low land along the rivers for cultivation, and Georgetown County was well suited for this with its five rivers: the Santee, Black, Pee Dee, Waccamaw, and Sampit. Slaves were essential to rice cultivation, not merely because labor was needed, but because of their knowledge of rice planting which they brought from Africa. The original rice seed, brought from Madagascar and introduced by Dr. Henry Woodward, was a low yielding rice. The planters worked steadily to improve the yield and eventually arrived at what became known as Carolina Gold, an international award winning seed.

It took approximately five years to clear an average swampy area of cypress and tupelo trees for rice planting. This was done with hand labor and with oxen wearing heavy leather boots to keep them from sinking in the mud. Earthen dams were constructed around swamps and water control structures, called trunks, were installed in the rice field banks. In Africa these were hollowed logs. Jonathan Lucas refined the "American" trunk. Trunkminders, usually a high ranking, trusted slave, controlled the water flow. The women and children combined the rice seed with mud to form clay balls, let them harden, and then planted them. The balls kept the seed from floating when the field was flooded. Rice growing using the tidal flow method was an exacting and intricate process. The harvested crop was tied in bundles and left on the bank to dry for a day or two before it was brought in for flailing and winnowing.

In 1840 the Georgetown District (County) produced nearly one-half of the total rice crop of the United States and economic prosperity continued for the plantation owners until the Civil War. The effects of the war were felt in every facet of life of the parishioners of Prince George Winyah Episcopal Church. A contemporary correspondent wrote that the church was used to stable horses. Miss Hannah Trapier sent a letter to the vestry stating her concern over the safe-keeping of the baptismal font, carpet, etc. but the vestry decided to keep them in the church. Miss Trapier's fears were not unfounded as the font was taken during this time of chaos. Fortunately it was later recovered from a yard where it was being used to pound rice and is now used for frequent baptisms.

Three major events ended rice culture in South Carolina. First, the Civil War freed the labor supply. Secondly, a series of bad storms and hurricanes salted the rice fields and damaged the rice field banks. The planters were not able to pay repeatedly to have the banks repaired. Thirdly, mechanical rice cultivation in Texas, Louisiana, and Arkansas produced rice more cheaply than the South Carolina planter could do it with paid hand labor. Rice cultivation, as it had been known, ended around 1910. It must be said that the

Baptismal font

fortunes amassed by rice production would not have been possible without the forced labor of slaves.

Slavery had been important to South Carolina since the first English settlement in 1670. Throughout the colonial period, thousands of West Africans were shipped to South Carolina and sold as slaves to both white and Negro masters. Most were captured by African slave traders, in a region that stretches between the present day nations of Gambia and Angola, and sold to European slave traders. The captives represented many African cultures, each with its own religion, customs, and language. These unwilling immigrants had little choice; they had to conform. Outwardly, most slaves tolerated bondage. Privately, black South Carolinians clung to their African heritage and cherished a desire for freedom. Having grown rice in Africa using the tidal flow system, the slaves brought with them invaluable knowledge of land and crops.

Despite harsh conditions under which they were forced to live, African-Americans created communities that combined African characteristics with those of their masters' culture. Of all slave societies in the New World, only the one established in the antebellum South grew through natural increase. Owners had much to gain by treating their "people" well. About 400,000 slaves were brought from Africa to the United States from the early 17th century until 1808; by 1860 the black population had increased to approximately 4 million.

Slave houses were small and used mainly for sleeping. Cooking and socializing were done outdoors. Sometimes two families shared a two room house, but most houses had one room with a sleeping loft for the children. During the winter everyone slept near the fire.

Artisans were a small, but valuable part, of the slave population. Owners found them essential to their plantations and businesses. From the beginning, Africans adapted their native skills to European-American demands. African crafts, such as pottery making, carpentry, blacksmithing, and boat building, were adjusted to conform to the practices in South Carolina. The work of slave artisans was usually credited to their owners. Sweetgrass baskets, or coiled grass baskets, a tradition in many parts of West Africa, have become part of the Lowcountry culture. The excellent, intricate woodworking, such as candlelight molding found in plantations and townhomes, can be attributed to the skilled hands of slaves.

Elisha Screven laid the plan for Georgetown in 1729 and began selling lots. In the 1828 Mills Atlas, the population for Georgetown District was listed as 1,830 white, 15,546 slave, and 227 free Negroes. Today the historic district comprises the area of the original town plan as shown on the inside cover of this book. The street names, with the exception of Bay Street being renamed Front Street, and Princess Street being renamed Prince Street, are still the same. Many of the houses are original to their present site. His anticipated "Church Street", however, never came to fruition. The Baptist Church was built on his lot 228 in 1804 but the other churches are spread throughout the city.

The area's history has been enriched by many prominent people. President George Washington visited Clifton Plantation in 1791 and addressed the people of Georgetown from the Robert Stewart house. President James Monroe was welcomed in 1821 at Prospect Hill (now Arcadia) on the Waccamaw with a red carpet rolled out to the river. Theodosia Burr Alston, daughter of Vice-President Aaron Burr, made her home at The Oaks Plantation, now a part of Brookgreen Gardens, after her marriage to Joseph Alston, who later became Governor of South Carolina. Brookgreen was the birth place of one of America's famous painters, Washington Allston. Joel R. Poinsett, while United States representative to Mexico, discovered and brought to South Carolina a plant which was later named in his honor: the poinsettia. He lived at White House on the Black River after retiring from government service and entertained President Martin Van Buren there. Robert F. W. Allston of Matanzas (now Chicora Wood) on the Pee Dee River served as Governor of South Carolina before the Civil War. President Grover Cleveland, as guest of the Annandale Gun Club, came for duck hunting and was feted by the citizens in 1894. Bernard Baruch, America's elder statesman and financier of the 20th century, entertained many notables at Hobcaw Barony, his home for many years. Among the guests were President Franklin D. Roosevelt, Sir Winston Churchill, General Mark Clark, and General Omar Bradley.

Front Street
Artist: Nancy Van Buren

Today, in the Historic District of Georgetown, which is listed on the National Register of Historic Places, more than 50 buildings and sites from the colonial period remain. Several of these townhomes are included on the annual Plantation Tour. Many of the plantation homes remain to give the area a real flavor of yesteryear and are offered on the tour as well. Most of the plantation homes and outbuildings are listed on the National Register of Historic Places.

Recognizing that Georgetown is a veritable treasure trove of history and charm, the women of Prince George Winyah, held their first plantation tour on April 11, 1947. Only the grounds and gardens of the plantations were viewed on this first occasion. Publicity was limited to local and state newspapers, and no advance tickets were sold. Tickets were $1.50. The first tour was such a great success that it was decided to repeat it the following year, but this time for two full days. Visitors were urged to bring a lunch and to spend the entire day touring.

The gardens were the focus of the early tours. Later, as more plantation homes were opened, the tours were less dependent on the gardens as the main attraction although nothing enhances a tour more than a beautiful spring day when the azaleas, camellias, bulbs, dogwood, and wisteria are in full bloom!

During the 1950's the plantation tours became a three day event, with plantation homes along the Waccamaw, Santee, Pee Dee/Black River and Sampit open to visitors. The church women made and offered box lunches at 60 cents. The tickets cost $2.00 a day or $5.00 for three days. Thankfully, a profit was made every year, surpassing $1,000.00 in 1953. In 1960 the tours were expanded to include some of the homes in Georgetown itself. Since that time 22 of Georgetown's finest old private residences have been included on tour.

Although tea had been served in homes in previous years, to mark the 25th anniversary of the plantation tours, an afternoon tea was held at the Winyah Indigo Society Hall by the church women. This has remained an annual event of the tours as a way to say "thank you" to our tour participants. The hall has welcomed weary guests with flowers, china, silver tea services, and prepared refreshments.

Eventually, the present pattern of the tours emerged with tours on Friday and Saturday. The need for volunteers, especially hosts and hostesses, has grown to mammoth proportions. The tours had a modest beginning of some nine plantation grounds for one afternoon, with a hostess or two at each place. In 2006, forty-six places were open requiring 300 volunteers. Although our church congregation has rapidly grown over the last several years, help for the tours is needed from the community. The people of the Georgetown area have generously provided their support, and the women of Prince George Winyah are grateful for every volunteer. Working together on the tours has promoted fellowship among the parishioners, as well as with those of the community.

It is a challenge each year to secure plantations, homes in Georgetown, map makers, map interpreters, typists, bookkeepers, printers, people to place the "tour marker" flags along roadsides, docents, facilitators at the Parish House, donors of banana nut bread, cookies, and cakes, people to prepare and dispense bag lunches, and the hosts and hostesses and cooks for the afternoon tea. The gracious owners of homes in town and on the plantations have consistently opened their homes and properties. They have welcomed hundreds of guests in a single day, year after year. On Saturday afternoon, when another year's work is ended, sighs of relief and satisfaction can be heard all over the parish. Preparations for the next tour begin on Monday.

The women of Prince George Winyah in answering God's call to help those in need, have tithed the proceeds from the tours to help many local causes, such as Hospice, Helping Hands, the Winyah Rescue Squad, The Rice Museum, Tara Hall Home for Boys, H.U.G.S. Program, Y.E.A. (Youth Enrichment Activities), Spencer Guerry Scholarship Fund, The Sunrise Program in Kenya, the Salvation Army Building Fund, The Inmate Fellowship Fund, Habitat for Humanity, the American Red Cross, and the Mental Health Association. Over the years, the remaining proceeds have been used for various church projects as well as maintaining the historical church buildings.

In 1947, the first cookbook was published by the women of Prince George Church to raise funds to refurbish the Parish House kitchen. It was a large endeavor achieved by a small committee consisting of Chairperson, Mrs. D. V. Richardson, Mrs. James R. Parker, and Mrs. Louis Overton. The Cook Book, with capital letters, as it was always referred to, was compiled from recipes of the best cooks in the community. Bound in a red, soft cover, it had 119 pages of recipes, interspersed with some advertisements, jingles by Mrs. W. W. Doar, and drawings by Mrs. Lewis Freeman. We have used many of the 1947 recipes in this book. You will find them designated by a pen and ink drawing of the Prince George clock and bell tower.

Some of the Committee members look over the new edition of THE CAROLINA LOWCOUNTRY COOKBOOK. Left to right: standing – Mrs. W.W. Doar, Mrs. D.V. Richardson, and Mrs. J.A. Kelley; seated – Mrs. Arthur Bailey, Mrs. A. Nelson Daunt, and Mrs. J.D. Feild, March 24, 1955.

In March, 1955, a second edition of the Cook Book was printed. A revised edition was printed in 1963 and again in 1975. In 1991, it was decided to use a picture of Prince George Winyah Church on the cover. The dedicated ladies who had transported The Carolina Lowcountry Cook Book of Georgetown, South Carolina, to various commercial outlets for those many years, now had the additional job of pasting the picture of the church on the covers.

Mrs. Herbert Smith's recipe for Peach-Date Chutney was selected for inclusion in a Time/Life publication, *The Good Cook*, in the volume called "Preserving", and Mrs. Joseph Bull's recipe for Brown Sugar Squares was included in the volume called "Biscuits." As was intended, proceeds from the cookbook over the past 60 years have been used to renovate the Parish House kitchen.

The new edition of our cookbook has taken two years to produce, and we will be forever indebted to the members of the parish for sharing their favorite, sometimes secret, recipes. Through a collaborative effort, we have met weekly and discussed the various areas of the book. Our typists and proofreaders have labored diligently to produce the manuscript. The original artwork displayed throughout the book has been graciously donated by the talented artists of our community. We featured as many of the plantations and houses in town as possible and regret that we could not locate paintings of them all. The fact that some were not featured lessens in no way their contribution to history. We are indebted to our rector, the Rev. Paul Fuener and our vestry for helping us with contributions and prayers.

As we celebrate the 60th anniversary of the founding of the Plantation Tours and the printing of our cookbook, we, the members of Prince George Winyah Parish, are grateful to God for our many blessings and we pray that He will continue to bless us and our community as He has abundantly done in the past.

The stained glass window behind the altar is English stained glass and was originally in St. Mary's Chapel at Hagley Plantation on the Waccamaw River. The chapel had been built by Plowden C. J. Weston for his slaves. After Weston's death, Mr. W. St. Julian Mazyck, who had inherited Hagley, gave the window to Prince George, along with a bell, clock, and a gold lined communion chalice. The estimated cost of putting up the clock and bell was $100.

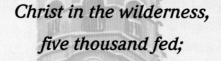

Christ in the wilderness,

five thousand fed;

Two small fishes and five loaves

of bread.

May the blessing of Him who made

the division

Rest upon us and our provision.

Amen.

Bishop Reindorp

WEDGEFIELD PLANTATION

Artist: Lu Hook

The history of Wedgefield Plantation begins in 1762 when Samuel Wragg secured 472 acres on the Black River owned formerly by John Waties. Wedgefield is bounded by Windsor and Mansfield Plantations. It passed through a succession of hands which include Joseph and Samuel Waties; Dr. Francis Parker of nearby Mansfield Plantation; the Reverend M. H. Lance; Joanna Gaillard; H. M. Haig; William, Elliott, and John Hazzard. In 1909, it was conveyed to Frederick Wentworth Ford of Georgetown. After living there for many years, the Fords sold the plantation in 1920 to James Scurry. Robert Goelet of Newport, Rhode Island, purchased this old plantation in 1935. He tore down the Wedgefield house to erect in its place the handsome dwelling of brick. Stripped of its white paint in the 1950's, the house features its warm natural brick exterior.

Like some plantations in Georgetown County, Wedgefield has been transformed into a country club and residential community. In 1988, a division of the property was made by the sale of the plantation residence, now called the Manor House, golf course, tennis courts, and pool operations. Today, Wedgefield Plantation Country Club is owned by the Marlowe family.

Samuel and Joseph Sampson House

Old Outdoor Kitchen   Artist: Pat Latstetter

The Samuel and Joseph Sampson house is located on Prince Street in Georgetown. The original part of the house on lot 91 consists of a two story weatherboard house and is one room deep with a central hall and stairway. It is a Georgian style house, likely built between 1740 and 1780. The Sampson brothers purchased the home around 1840. It was later resold to the Ward family in 1866.

It has hand hewn sills and joists. The braced frame construction with hewn and pegged hanging joists attest to the pre-Revolutionary date. The interior architecture has much of the original fabric, but the succession of owners have altered some features and added others. The 9/9 window sashes have poured glass panes and wide muntins.

The original kitchen was built about ten years before the house and still stands on the property. It is a one and one-half story cypress frame building with a gable end roof. The ground floor contains two rooms separated by a massive central brick chimney with double faced cooking fireplaces. The loft has a two-sided fireplace also. Few examples of this type of kitchen building remain in South Carolina making it a significant example of service architecture.

This house is listed on the National Register of Historic Places.

DR. CHARLES FYFFE HOUSE

Harbor House   Artist: Doris Athey

The Dr. Charles Fyffe House is located on Front Street in Georgetown. Dr. Charles Fyffe, a Scottish physician, came to South Carolina in 1748 and soon became one of Georgetown's leading citizens. He was a charter member of the Charleston Library Society and one of the first stewards of the Winyah Indigo Society. In 1763, he bought the lot on which this house was erected. When colonists rebelled against England, Fyffe remained loyal to Great Britain. As a consequence, he was banished, his property confiscated and sold, and he never regained his home.

HARBOR HOUSE AND INDEPENDENT SEAFOOD

Artist: Johnie Cowan

The house is a two and one-half story Georgian style. The main part of the house is under the pyramidal roof supported by a king post trussing system. It is a braced frame construction with massive timbers, and mortise and tenon joints. The unusual floor plan has a main parlor with a paneled dado and main field characteristic of the late Georgian period (1765-1811) and the Federal period (1780-1850). The cornice has roll-and-bead and candlestick molding, but the original mantel has been replaced. The dining room features candlelight molding with beaded molding below it. This room also has a replacement mantel. Both the kitchen and the smaller parlor behind the main parlor have simple dado and plain field, as do the rooms upstairs. The mantels in these two rooms and in the upstairs bedrooms are most typical of wooden mantels of the Federal period. The house is a fascinating example of the transition in architectural tastes of the residents between 1770 and 1800.

The house is owned and operated as the Harbor House Bed and Breakfast by Meg Tarbox Williams.

KAMINSKI HOUSE MUSEUM

Artist: Lon Calhoun

In 1769, Paul Trapier II, a widower about to remarry, built this house and conveyed it to his spinster daughter, Elizabeth, along with two lots and thirty-two slaves. Elizabeth eventually married Sheriff Edward Martin, but the two were childless. Her brother, Paul, died quite young leaving three sons and a daughter. Elizabeth took them in and added a one-story addition to the rear of the house. She eventually passed the house on to her niece, Magdalene, who married the first intendant of Georgetown, John Keith. There were many owners before 1931 when Harold and Julia Kaminski purchased the house.

Originally the Kaminski house was a three-story single house with nine-over-nine windows and beaded clapboard siding. George Congden greatly enlarged the house with additions at the rear and both sides. Most of the original woodwork is still visible. The stairway, newel, balusters, as well as the dado in the central hall appear to be original to the house. The doors to these rooms are also original, with self-closing hinges that were popular in the eighteenth and nineteenth centuries. In the enlarged dining room, it is possible to distinguish the first cornice in the older part of the room from that in the later extension of that room. The dining room also has a good Federal mantel, and it appears that an original overmantel may have been removed. The first rooms on the second floor have early mantels and six-panel doors with HL hinges. The detailing of the second floor is much more reserved than that of the first, but is still classical in feeling.

Harold and Julia Pyatt Kaminski purchased the house in 1931 and made a number of additions and changes to the house. Among these were the extension of the dining room and living room by enclosing the wrap-around porches on the northern and southern ends of the house and bricking the walls. The Kaminskis also embellished the interior of their home with a notable collection of exceptional antiques. Many of these were from a collection amassed by Mr. Kaminski's mother, Rose. After Julia Kaminski's death, the house and its furnishings were willed to the City of Georgetown in honor of her husband and his mother to be used as an Historic House Museum.

THE WESTON HOUSE/PELICAN INN

Artist: Gail Joley

Plowden Charles Jennett Weston (1819-1864) received five acres on Pawley's Island from Peter Fraser in 1846. His beach residence was erected by the time of the 1858 plat of the island was made. The house was built by Renty Tucker, a slave on Hagley Plantation, one of the most talented carpenters in All Saints' Parish. The family called this house "Weston's Toyland". Elizabeth Collins, the English woman employed by the Westons, wrote of the house in 1860, "I can only compare this building to a castle so lofty that we could find a cool place almost in any part of the house."

The Greek Revival style house is a two and one-half story gable end building with cornice returns on the gable ends. The first story has a recessed porch which appears once to have been on all sides of the building, portions of which are now enclosed. A small one story gable end kitchen building is now joined to the house by a porch on the northern facade.

Weston's widow conveyed the house to William St. Julian Mazyck in 1864 and it remained in that family until 1901. In 1887, it was operated as the Ocean View Hotel. In 1901, the Atlantic Coast Lumber Company purchased it for use by company employees for vacations.

It is presently owned by Mrs. Theodore R. Evans (Hope) and is operated as Evans' Pelican Inn.

THE WEDGE PLANTATION

Artist: Honley

The Wedge Plantation derives its name from its triangular shape of the property which widens from a narrow entrance to a broad frontage on the South Santee River. Although it has been enlarged over the years with the addition of tracts of land from several other plantations, the estate has, nevertheless, managed to retain its characteristic conformation.

For many years, The Wedge was owned by William Lucas, son of Jonathan Lucas inventor of the first successful rice-pounding mill. This invention did for the grain what Whitney's gin invention did for cotton. In 1826, William Lucas built the house which was owned and lived in by his family for a full century.

The spacious four-storied house is basically of Georgian design with simplified adaptations from the Greek Revival style prevalent and popular at the time of its construction. It consists of a central block flanked by symmetrical wings which contain polygonal rooms. The ground floor is of brick imported as ballast from England and Holland in the trading ships of the era, and the rooms above have the high ceilings and generous proportions that are so well suited to the climate of the Lowcountry. Although extensively restored and renovated in the 1920's, the house still has most of its original features, including the hand carved finials above the front columns. The house is now owned by the University of South Carolina and is leased as a hunting lodge.

CHARLOTTE J. ATKINSON HOUSE

Artist: Unknown

The earliest recorded owner of this house located on Prince Street in Georgetown was Charlotte J. Atkinson. In her will of 1820 she bequeathed the house to her daughter, Mary Pyatt Allston. The property remained in the Allston family until 1898, when they sold it and the lot to D. T. Smith.

Built in the Federal style, this house was one room deep with a central hallway. The house contained two parlors on the first floor and two bedrooms on the second floor. The property had a one-story addition at the rear of the house soon after it was completed, and had a one-story front porch until 1899. The age of this part of the house is testified by framing timbers which are band sawn, indicating that this section was constructed before 1840. Between 1899 and 1908 drastic changes were made to the house. By 1908 it had become a two-story double house with a two-story porch on the rear and also a two-story porch on the front.

These changes dramatically altered its exterior appearance. Once a gable-end house with a low front porch, it had become a low-hip roofed house with the appearance of a Folk Victorian style c. 1870-1910. The doorways and windows throughout the first and second floors exhibit identical reeded surrounds with ornamental corner blocks. The staircase is original and features a heavy turned newel post and unusual balusters. Much of the woodwork remains, as well as the six-over-six windows with thin muntins. Of particular interest are the mantels in the front rooms on the first floor. These mantels were brought from the overseers house at Rosemont Plantation.

MARY MAN HOUSE

Artist: Jacquie Harris

The Mary Man house is located on Front Street in Georgetown. The land upon which this house stands was first deeded to William Waties in 1737. It was successively owned by Robert Lucas, Thomas Lynch, and James Gordon, who sold the lot to Mary Man in 1772. Mary, the daughter of Dr. John Man of Mansfield Plantation on the Black River, was a twenty-four year old spinster when she acquired the property. Using lumber and labor from that rice plantation, she constructed the house probably between 1772-1776. In 1785, she married Archibald Taylor. The couple had two children, John Man Taylor, who never married, and, Anna Marie Taylor Lance, whose daughter, Esther Jane Lane Read, sold the house to Benjamin Ingell Hazard family in 1876. He was the great-grandfather of Patrick J. Doyle who along with his wife, Patricia, have renovated this impressive house that continues to serve as their residence.

This handsome Georgian style dwelling has original clapboard sheathing, pediment and decorative dental molding, and fretwork under the eaves, with hipped roof and a double-tiered piazza. The remarkable thing about the house is that it is historically intact. The heart of pine floors, most of the doors, the woodwork (except some in the hall and dining room), much of the plaster, and seven of the eight hearths are all original. The rear addition and back porch date from 1912.

The east and west drawing rooms feature identical Georgian paneled fireplace walls typical of the period with an eared flip around the mantel shelves. The woodwork motif in the east room is candlelight, while the west room has a handsome demilune cornice; both have plain paneled dado with simple plain field above the chair rail. The hall stairs are original, and feature turned balusters, a square newel post, pendants, and fine decorative hand carving on the wave brackets.

Theodosia Burr Alston, daughter of former vice-president Aaron Burr, is said to have danced in the spacious second floor ballroom (now bedroom and hall) the night before she embarked on her ill-fated voyage in 1812.

THE RICE MUSEUM

Rice Museum Town Clock
Artist: Dian Hammett

As early as 1788, the site at Screven and Front Streets in Georgetown was the location of the town's open-air market. This brick building replaces an earlier wooden structure that was torn down in 1841 to make a fire break during a fire that threatened the businesses on the 700 block of Front Street. In 1842, the entire block, including the market and adjacent Kaminski Hardware Store, was rebuilt. The clock tower was added in 1845. In February 1865, when Federal troops occupied Georgetown, the town council signed surrender papers in this building. The second floor of the Town Clock was used as the town hall prior to 1970.

When the Georgetown County Historical Commission purchased the Town Clock building from the City of Georgetown, they restored the structure. It reopened in May of 1970 as the Rice Museum in celebration of the South Carolina Tricentennial. The clockworks in the tower were made operational again in 1975.

Lafayette Park surrounds the Rice Museum and is a refreshing urban green space on the banks of the Sampit River. The Lowcountry Herb Society maintains a sensory garden of indigenous plants in the park.

ROBERT STEWART HOUSE

Artist: Myrna J. McMahon

The Robert Stewart House is located on Front Street in Georgetown. The first owner of Lot 220 was Robert Stewart, a landowner and planter. The original part of the house was built between 1740 and 1776 and is a two and one-half story Georgian structure over a raised basement. The exterior walls are fifteen inches thick, and the joints are hewn-and-pegged 10x3-inch timbers.

The house is composed of two sections with the original portion, c.1750, facing the Sampit River and the later addition, c.1810, facing the street. The house is stucco over brick and is Georgetown's only brick residence with a pre-Revolutionary date. The unique exterior features two semicircular bays on the first floor garden front. The interior contains fine woodwork, some of which is original.

In 1787, Daniel Tucker purchased the house from Stewart's estate, and renovations gave the house a more Federal or Adam appearance. The house was stuccoed and scored to resemble stone. Stucco lintels and keystones were created above the original nine-over-nine windows. The ornamentation had been kept to a minimum, but decorative plaster moldings were added to the new rooms, the entrance hall, and the southern parlor. The porch facing the river was probably added around 1820. The porch facing Front Street was a later addition.

The house passed to Benjamin Allston in 1824 and remained in the possession of that family until 1979.

It is now owned by The National Society of the Colonial Dames of America in the State of South Carolina and leased to the city of Georgetown which uses it as administrative offices for the adjacent Kaminski House Museum and for special events.

FRANCIS WITHERS FEDERAL HOUSE

Artist: Connie Bull

The earliest documented ownership of this Georgetown house, located on Cannon Street, appears in the 1841 will of Francis Withers.

Francis Withers (1769-1847) was the son of Charleston bricklayer, James Withers, who in 1736 received a grant of 120 acres on Georgetown Creek (now the Sampit River). Francis later became the owner of seven plantations on the Sampit River. Although he was an Anglican, Withers became a supporter of the Methodist Mission To Slaves and built a meeting place for them on Friendfield Plantation. In his will, he left the property on the south side of Princess (now Prince) Street to be used as a residence for the officiating preacher for a period of 10 years or until the owners of Friendfield Plantation and the Negroes objected to the continuation of services. He also left the land on the southwest corner of Princess (Prince) and Cannon Streets to the Winyah Indigo Society, of which he was a member, for the building of the present hall of the Society.

Mr. Withers left the Cannon Street house to his daughter, Mrs. Elizabeth Wayne. Mrs. Wayne died before Mr. Withers, however, so a codicil in 1845 bequeathed the property to her daughter, Mrs. Eleanor Gregg. By 1860, the house began a series of changes in ownership, ending in 1926 with its purchase by the late Joseph L. Bull, Jr. He and his wife, the former Emily Bailey, were among the first in this century to value and restore a historic Georgetown townhouse. Mrs. Bull made this her home until her death in 1993. The house was inherited by her son, Clayton M. Bull, who oversaw the extensive restoration. He now resides in the house with his wife, Margaret (Connie) Thomas Bull.

The Francis Withers House is an example of an Early Classical Revival style (1770-1850) raised cottage. The portico dominates the front facade, the simple columns in the Roman or Tuscan style, the semicircular fanlight in the gable, and the raised basement are all characteristics of this style. The interior in this style house often exhibits the Federal or Adams style of their contemporaries, and this is evident in the Francis Withers house.

Mansfield Plantation

Mansfield Plantation, located on the Black River, reflects more clearly than any other the typical rice plantation. It dates from 1718 when John Green received a land grant. In 1756, Mrs. Susannah LaRouche Man, then a recent widow of Dr. John Man, purchased the property and named it for her family. Mrs. Man left the property to her son, John Man Taylor, in 1803. A Harvard graduate, Taylor lived at Mansfield and oversaw 125 slaves. He died in 1823, leaving Mansfield to his sister, Anna Marie Taylor Lance. Anna Marie and her second husband, Josias Allston Jr. and their two daughters, Mary Taylor and Esther Jane, lived at Mansfield for 25 years. Mary Taylor married Dr. Francis Simon Parker of Charleston in 1836. He gave up his medical career to become a rice planter at Mansfield. The plantation remained in the Parker family until 1912 when it was purchased by Charles W. Tuttle of Auburn, New York, to be a winter home and hunt club. In 1931, Mansfield was sold to Colonel and Mrs. R. L. Montgomery of Ardrossan, Pennsylvania. They worked diligently to preserve and beautify the buildings and grounds. Roof tiles were imported from Cuba. Decorative ironwork by Charleston artisan, Thomas Pinckney, enhances the flankers, and the brick fan motif makes the terrace unique. A basement was added to the main house. The small schoolbuilding in the front and the old outdoor kitchen to the rear were converted into guest houses.

Mansfield Street, which forms the plantation avenue, is lined with live oak trees that shelter the old slave chapel and some of the original slave cabins. The plantation is noted for this restored slave street.

Mansfield Schoolhouse   Artist: Lib Ferdon

Mansfield Winnowing House   Artist: Janet Baril

Mansfield also has the county's only surviving original winnowing house which is located near the canal. Raised from the ground, the winnowing house was used for the sifting of chaff from the rice. As the grain was poured through the opening in the floor, the wind would carry off the light chaff while the heavier rice fell into containers.

In November, 1970, Mansfield was purchased by Mr. and Mrs. Wilbur Smith. Their daughter, Sally Smith, sold Mansfield to John Rutledge Parker and his wife, Sallie Middleton Parker in April, 2004, returning Mansfield once again to the Parker family after an absence of 92 years. Mansfield is operated as a Bed and Breakfast, and is on the National Register of Historic Places.

THE SPRINGS-MARING HOUSE

Artist: Lori Maring Hutchins

The Springs-Maring house is located on Prince Street in Georgetown. It was built in 1882 by Holmes Gardner Springs. The original transom over the door had his initials carved in the glass. Unfortunately, a generic one has replaced the original transom that remains in the possession of a descendant of Mr. Springs.

The original structure had a second floor porch, but this was removed and replaced by the present six columns in the late 1930's or early 1940's. The design was inspired by the famous movie, Gone with the Wind, a common facelift that swept the South after the release of the movie.

Around 1940, the house came into possession of the Francis Stokes Collins family. It remained in the Collins family until 1975 when it passed into the hands of Mr. and Mrs. Joel Burdette, who later sold it in 1980 to Barry Price.

In 1995, the home was sold to its present owners, Circuit Judge David H. Maring and his wife, Judy.

HOPSEWEE PLANTATION

Artist: Unknown

Hopsewee is located on the North Santee River. Only four families have owned this plantation although it was built almost forty years before the Revolutionary War. It is a preservation rather than a restoration.

Hopsewee, a typical lowcountry rice plantation house of the early 18th century has four rooms opening into a wide central hall on each floor, a full brick cellar, and attic rooms. The hand carved moldings are different in each room with one and one- half inch thick random width heart pine floors. Constructed on a brick foundation covered by scored tabby, the house is built of black cypress, which probably accounts for the fact that it is basically the same house Thomas Lynch II built over 250 years ago.

The two cypress shingled outbuildings were used as kitchens. Each outbuilding has a large fireplace on one side of the chimney and a double fireplace on the other. The division allowed for a simultaneous hot fire and a simmering fire. The construction of these outbuildings mirrors the West Indies influence on the early colonists.

Thomas Lynch II and Thomas Lynch, Jr. were distinguished political figures. They were the only father and son serving in the 2nd Continental Congress. Thomas Lynch, Jr. signed the Declaration of Independence. Thomas Lynch II, however, died before he was able to add his name to this historic document on which a space was left for his signature.

Hopsewee was placed on the National Historic Register in 1971 and is now the home of Mr. and Mrs. Franklin D. Beattie.

Prince George Winyah Parish   Artist: Gertrude Bull

PRAYER OF
THE WOMEN OF THE CHURCH

Almighty God, our Heavenly Father, bless we pray Thee, our work for the extension of Thy kingdom, and make us so thankful for the precious gift to us of Thy beloved Son, that we may pray fervently, labor diligently, and give liberally to make Him known to all nations as their Savior and their King, through the same Jesus Christ, our Lord.

Amen.

Arcadia Plantation
Artist: Danny McLaughlin

Arcadia, as it is known today, is located on the Waccamaw Neck. It was once seven prosperous rice plantations. Among these was Prospect Hill, where the original dwelling still remains.

Originally granted to Percival Pawley in 1711, the tract stayed in Pawley's hands for nearly sixty years. It was then acquired by Joseph Allston, known locally as Joseph of the Oaks. Joseph's son, Thomas, is believed to have built the beautiful house which can still be seen today. It is said to be an exact copy of the house built at Clifton Plantation by Thomas' older brother, William, where he had the great honor of entertaining President George Washington during his southern tour of 1791.

Thomas died suddenly in 1795, leaving his widow his plantation and a house frame. Mary Allston then married Benjamin Huger II. In 1819, President James Monroe was a guest of the Hugers at Prospect Hill. Shortly after the death of Mr. Huger, his widow sold the plantation to Colonel Joshua John Ward, who passed it to his son, Benjamin Huger Ward. With the loss of the Civil War, the place was partitioned and eventually lost to foreclosure.

In 1906, the property was purchased by Dr. Isaac Edward Emerson, who modernized the house, built the two wings on either side of the house, acquired the adjacent plantations, and named the entire tract Arcadia. Upon his death in 1931, the plantation passed to his grandson, George Vanderbilt. Since 1961, it has been the home of Mr. Vanderbilt's daughter, Lucille V. Pate and her family.

In 1970 and again in 1985, portions of the outlying plantations were sold. Standing on the grounds of Arcadia Plantation is St. Anne's Church which was erected by Major Huger who served in the Revolutionary Army in the late eighteenth century and was used as a hospital for slaves until the close of the Civil War in 1865. It was rebuilt by Dr. Emerson for the African-Americans of Arcadia in 1927. Behind the altar there was a small school. This school was in full operation until 1956. Arcadia Plantation is on the National Register of Historic Places.

CHIPOTLE SWISS CHEESE FONDUE

THE MELTING POT IN MYRTLE BEACH, SC

4	ounces white wine	2	teaspoons finely diced chipotle peppers
1	teaspoon minced garlic		
2	cups shredded Swiss cheese, or to taste	2	teaspoons minced shallots
	Fresh cracked black pepper	1	teaspoon chopped parsley, for garnish

Combine, in order listed, all ingredients except parsley in fondue pot. Stir until smooth. Garnish with parsley and serve with fresh bread, carrots, cauliflower and celery.

Yield: 2-4 servings.

CRAB AND ARTICHOKE DIP

BROOKGREEN GARDENS, MURRELLS INLET, SC

3	(14 ounce) cans of artichoke hearts	1	cup shredded mozzarella cheese
1	(12 ounce) can crab claw meat	½	cup grated Parmesan cheese
½	cup mayonnaise		Paprika

Preheat oven to 350°. Spray 9x13-inch pan with cooking spray. Combine above ingredients in the pan. Sprinkle with paprika and bake for 10-15 minutes.

Yield: 15 (4 ounce) servings.

MASTER *of men, Thou hast given us work to do.* *Give us strength to do it well, on time, and cheerfully, for Thy Name's sake. Amen*

A PRAYER TO BLESS THIS FOOD

Our heavenly Father, we thank you for all the good things of life; for good food, for good friends, for good fellowship. Bless this food to the nourishment of our bodies, bless this fellowship to the nourishment of souls, and bless all those we love now absent from us; we ask through Jesus Christ our Lord. Amen

SHRIMP ROLL

3 (8 ounce) packages cream cheese, softened

3 pounds shrimp, boiled, peeled, and ground

1 medium onion, grated

Season with red pepper

Worcestershire to taste

Chopped pecans

Dried parsley

Thoroughly mix first 5 ingredients. Roll into ball; then roll ball in chopped pecans or parsley. Slice and serve on crackers.

Yield: 45-50 servings.

Dorothy Ross

CALIFORNIA CHEESE LACE

Vegetable cooking spray

8   ounces Monterey Jack cheese, cut into ½ inch squares, ¼ inch thick

Preheat oven to 350°. Spray one or more baking sheets with vegetable cooking spray. Arrange squares of cheese on baking sheet, allowing a 2-inch border around edges of pan as well as between each square.

Bake until cheese is melted and bubbly, 5-7 minutes. Let cool on baking sheet until just set, about 2 minutes; then use a wire spatula to remove them to a wire rack to cool and harden. Serve at room temperature.

Yield: 80 pieces.

Baking parchment paper may also be used instead of spraying a baking sheet.

GEORGETOWN SHRIMP DIP

HARBOR HOUSE BED AND BREAKFAST, GEORGETOWN, SC

3   pounds small shrimp

2   lemons, squeezed for juice

2   tablespoons Worcestershire sauce

Hot pepper sauce to taste

Grated onion juice

Salt and pepper to taste

Mayonnaise to spread

Boil shrimp with plenty of salt. Peel and devein. Grind shrimp in food processor. Mix in lemon juice, Worcestershire sauce, hot pepper sauce, onion juice, and salt and pepper. Add mayonnaise to make spreading consistency.

Hellmann's mayonnaise was recommended for this recipe.

FAMOUS CRAB DIP

TRAWLERS RESTAURANT, MT. PLEASANT, SC

1¼ cups mayonnaise

1   cup fresh crabmeat

½   cup finely grated Cheddar cheese

1   teaspoon horseradish

4   tablespoons French dressing

Mix all ingredients. Refrigerate overnight. Serve with crackers. For more tang, use more horseradish and/or more French dressing.

Yield: 3 cups.

CRAB DIP

DRUNKEN JACK'S, MURRELLS INLET, SC

1	(8 ounce) package cream cheese, softened	½	cup shredded Cheddar cheese
1	pound lump crabmeat	1	tomato, seeded and diced
¼	cup cooking sherry	½	cup thinly cut carrots
½	teaspoon seafood seasoning	2	scallion stems, chopped Paprika
¼	small red onion, finely diced		

Place softened cream cheese in mixing bowl and whip. Fold in crabmeat, sherry, seafood seasoning and onion until well-blended. Fold in Cheddar cheese. Use tomatoes, carrots, scallions and paprika for garnish. Serve with crackers.

Yield: 10 servings.

HAM AND PICKLED OKRA SPIRALS

1	(16 ounce) jar hot, pickled okra	1	(6½ ounce) jar sun-dried tomato and basil spreadable cheese (or any cream cheese)
1	(10 ounce) package honey ham, thinly sliced		

Cut tips from both ends of the okra. Stand upright to drain on paper towels for at least 30 minutes. Prepare entire jar at one time. Wipe moisture from both sides of a single ham slice with paper towel and spread entire surface with a thin layer of cream cheese. Position ham with the long edge in front of you. Lay okras horizontally on the ham, end to end. You will use 2-3 pieces of okra or whatever it takes to cover the entire length of the ham slice. Bring ham up over okra and roll to the opposite edge. Repeat until the ham and okra run out. You will have approximately 8 rolls. Wrap in plastic wrap and refrigerate at least 1 hour. This makes slicing easier. To serve, slice in ½ inch rounds. This can be done hours ahead of serving, then cover.

Draining the okra and wiping off the ham are important steps to prevent the cream cheese from being runny. The unsliced rolls can be prepared up to 2 days in advance.

This sounds strange, but the spirals are great!!

SAUTÉED CAROLINA SHRIMP & HERBED COUNTRY SAUSAGE

Royal Oak Pub, Murrells Inlet, SC

½ *pound seasoned bulk sausage with sage, cayenne and nutmeg added*

1 teaspoon clarified butter

20 shrimp, peeled and deveined

1 teaspoon spice mix (see below)

3 tablespoons scallions, chopped

1 tablespoon Irish whiskey

2 tablespoons whole butter

2 cups cooked grits (stone ground speckled)

Form flavored sausage into balls about the size of nickels. Sauté in a skillet with clarified butter until almost done. Add shrimp and spice mix and continue to sauté approximately 2 minutes. Add scallions and toss, cooking about 1 minute. Deglaze with whiskey and ignite. After flames have subsided, add whole butter, stir, and pour over hot grits. Serve immediately.

Yield: 4 servings as an appetizer.

Spice Mix
Salt, Dried thyme, Oregano, Basil, Black pepper, White pepper, Crushed red pepper flakes

Deglazing is a cooking procedure used to dissolve fragments that remain in a roasting or frying pan. This is done by heating, then adding a liquid so as to make a sauce.

APPLE AND PEAR SLICES

Dip apple and pear slices in solution of lemon juice and water to keep them from turning brown.

OYSTERS ROCKEFELLER

2	dozen oysters	1	teaspoon Worcestershire
¾	cup soft breadcrumbs		sauce
¼	cup melted butter		Rock salt
1	cup finely chopped fresh	¼	cup grated Parmesan
	spinach		cheese
¼	cup chopped onion		Lemon wedges
1	teaspoon seasoned salt		Fresh parsley

Preheat oven to 400°. Rinse oysters in cold water. Shuck, reserving deep-half of shells. Drain oysters in colander and set aside. Combine breadcrumbs, and butter; set aside. Combine spinach, onion, seasoned salt, Worcestershire sauce and set aside. Cover bottom of broiler pan with rock salt and place oyster shells on top of salt. Place oysters in each shell and cover with spinach mixture and cheese. Top with bread crumb mixture. Bake for 15 minutes. Broil 4-inches from heat for 2 minutes or until browned. Garnish with lemon and parsley.

Yield: 8-12 servings.

WARMED CRANBERRY BRIE CHEESE

1	(16 ounce) round Brie cheese	½	teaspoon ground nutmeg
		¼	cup chopped pecans, toasted
1	(16 ounce) can whole-berry cranberry sauce		Crackers
¼	cup firmly packed brown sugar		Apple and pear slices, to garnish
2	tablespoons spiced rum		

Preheat oven to 500°. Trim rind from top of Brie, leaving a ⅓-inch border on top. Place Brie on a baking sheet. Stir together cranberry sauce, brown sugar, rum, and nutmeg; spread mixture evenly over top of Brie. Sprinkle evenly with pecans. Bake for 5 minutes. Serve with assorted crackers and apple and pear slices.

Yield: 12-15 servings.

Two tablespoons orange juice may be substituted for spiced rum.

CHAMPAGNE CHEESE BALL

½	pound sharp Cheddar cheese, grated	¼	cup finely chopped onion
2	tablespoons butter	1	garlic clove, minced
2	(3 ounce) packages cream cheese, softened	1	teaspoon Worcestershire sauce
½	cup champagne (dry white wine may be substituted)	¼	teaspoon salt

In a bowl, combine first 3 ingredients until thoroughly mixed. Gradually add champagne, stirring all the while. Stir in the onion, garlic, Worcestershire sauce, and salt. Cover the mixture and chill for 1 hour.

CHEESE BALL TOPPING

1¼	cups finely chopped walnuts	1	teaspoon paprika
1	tablespoon chopped parsley	1	teaspoon chili powder
		1	teaspoon curry powder
		1	teaspoon dill

On a sheet of waxed paper, form the mixture into a ball. In a small dish, combine the topping ingredients. Spread the mixture onto the waxed paper, and roll the ball in it until thoroughly coated. Wrap the ball in plastic wrap and chill for 3 hours or until ready to serve. Serve it with plain crackers.

DIABLO CHICKEN WINGS

3	pounds chicken wings	½	teaspoon garlic powder
1	tablespoon coarse salt	1	teaspoon onion powder
1	teaspoon paprika	1	teaspoon lemon pepper
½	teaspoon red pepper flakes		

Cut off tips of chicken wings. Place seasonings in plastic bag and mix well. Add wings to bag and toss. Grill or broil 8 minutes on each side.

CRAB SPREAD

12 ounces cream cheese, softened

2 tablespoons Worcestershire sauce

2 tablespoons lemon juice

2 tablespoons grated onion

1 cup chili sauce

2 teaspoons prepared horseradish (optional)

¾ pound fresh crabmeat

¼ cup chopped parsley

Combine cream cheese, Worcestershire sauce, lemon juice, and onion. Put in quiche dish. Top with layer of chili sauce mixed with horseradish, if desired; then a layer of crabmeat. Sprinkle with parsley. Chill. Serve with crackers.

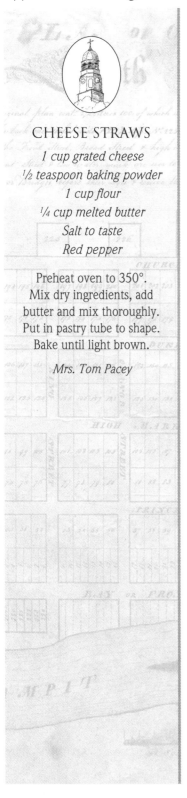

CHEESE STRAWS

1 cup grated cheese
½ teaspoon baking powder
1 cup flour
¼ cup melted butter
Salt to taste
Red pepper

Preheat oven to 350°.
Mix dry ingredients, add
butter and mix thoroughly.
Put in pastry tube to shape.
Bake until light brown.

Mrs. Tom Pacey

FOOD PROCESSOR CHEESE STRAWS

3	cups all-purpose flour	2	(10 ounce) blocks of extra sharp Cheddar cheese
1	teaspoon cayenne pepper	1	cup butter
1½	teaspoons baking powder	1	tablespoon hot pepper sauce
1	teaspoon salt		

Preheat oven to 350°. Sift first 4 ingredients twice. Set aside. Grate cheese in food processor. Add butter and hot pepper sauce and process. Add flour mixture while processing, a little at a time. Put into a cookie press and press onto cookie sheets. Bake for 15-20 minutes.

MUSHROOM CROUSTADES

SHELLS

24	slices thin-sliced white bread	**Butter, softened**

Preheat oven to 400°. Brush 24 tiny muffin cups liberally with the butter. Cut 2-inch rounds from the bread. Carefully fit them into muffin cups to make little cups. Bake for 10 minutes. Watch carefully. Allow to cool and remove to cookie sheet.

FILLING

3	tablespoons chopped shallots	3-4	dashes cayenne pepper
½	pound mushrooms, chopped	1	tablespoon chopped parsley
4	tablespoons butter	1½	tablespoons chopped chives
2	tablespoons flour	½	teaspoon lemon juice
1	cup cream		Grated Parmesan cheese
1½	teaspoons salt		

Sauté shallots and mushrooms in butter until moisture is cooked away (10-15 minutes). Sprinkle flour over mixture and stir well. Add cream and bring to a boil; simmer one minute. Remove from heat. Add salt, cayenne pepper, parsley, chives, lemon juice; mix and cool. When ready to serve, fill cups with mixture, sprinkle with Parmesan cheese, and heat in moderate oven for 10 minutes.

Yield: 24 servings.

MUSHROOM CAPS STUFFED WITH CRAB

see recipe box for recipe *combined this with another*

16	large mushrooms	3	tablespoons Italian parsley
9	tablespoons minced onion	⅓	cup dried breadcrumbs
4	tablespoons olive oil	3	tablespoons fresh thyme
3	tablespoons unsalted butter		Salt and pepper to taste
3	cloves garlic, minced	⅓	cup dry white wine
½	cup crabmeat	⅓	cup Parmesan cheese

Old Bay

Preheat oven to 350°. Clean mushrooms. Remove and chop stems. Sauté onions in oil with 3 tablespoons butter over high heat until onions are clear. Add garlic and mushroom stems and sauté until wilted. Add crabmeat, stirring for 5 minutes. Stir in parsley, breadcrumbs, and seasonings. Pile into caps and put in casserole dish. Pour wine into dish. Sprinkle with Parmesan cheese and white wine. Bake for 15 minutes. Pour off wine and serve hot.

Yield: 8-10 servings.

Note: Try precooking mushrooms a little in a seasoned broth

STILTON AND WALNUT WAFERS

KUDZU BAKERY MARKET, GEORGETOWN, SC

3	cups all-purpose flour	1	pound Stilton Blue Cheese, cold and broken into small pieces
1	cup butter		
1	teaspoon salt		
1	cup walnut pieces	⅓	cup milk

Preheat oven to 350°. In mixing bowl combine flour, butter, and salt. Mix thoroughly. Add walnuts and continue to mix. Add cheese and mix. Add milk and mix until dough just comes together. Turn out on table and roll into logs. Wrap and refrigerate or freeze. Spray cookie sheet with vegetable cooking spray. Slice chilled dough into thin wafers and place on cookie sheet. Bake for 12-15 minutes.

CHEESE BISCUITS WITH PECANS

1 cup butter

2 cups shredded extra sharp Cheddar cheese

2 cups flour

1 teaspoon salt

½ teaspoon cayenne pepper

1 cup chopped pecans

Preheat oven to 400°. Combine all ingredients in large bowl. Mix together with hands until blended. Roll between palms into balls the size of large marbles and flatten slightly. Arrange on cookie sheets and chill thoroughly. Bake about 11-12 minutes.

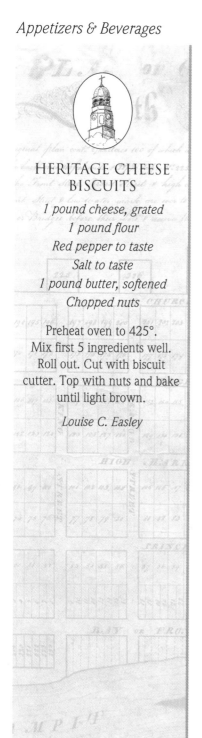

HERITAGE CHEESE BISCUITS

1 pound cheese, grated
1 pound flour
Red pepper to taste
Salt to taste
1 pound butter, softened
Chopped nuts

Preheat oven to 425°.
Mix first 5 ingredients well.
Roll out. Cut with biscuit
cutter. Top with nuts and bake
until light brown.

Louise C. Easley

CHEESE BISCUITS WITH CRISP RICE CEREAL

1½ cups butter, softened	2½ cups flour
12 ounces sharp Cheddar cheese, grated	2½ cups crisp rice cereal
	¼ teaspoon cayenne pepper

Preheat oven to 350°. Mix butter with grated cheese. Add flour slowly and mix. Add cereal, mix well. Add pepper. Roll into small balls and put on ungreased cookie sheet. Press flat. Bake 15-20 minutes until golden brown.

SHRIMP APPETIZER

1 pound shrimp, cooked and peeled	¼ cup water
1 (10½ ounce) can tomato soup	1 cup mayonnaise
1 (8 ounce) package cream cheese	¾ cup chopped celery
2 envelopes unflavored gelatin	¾ cup chopped spring onions or yellow onions
	½ cup chopped bell pepper

Grind shrimp and set aside. Heat soup to boil. Add cream cheese and let melt in soup. Dissolve gelatin in water. Add gelatin to soup and stir until dissolved. Fold in remaining ingredients and the shrimp. Pour into greased 6-cup mold and refrigerate until set. Serve with crackers.

Yield: 40 servings when served as an appetizer.

Yield: 6-8 servings when served on lettuce as a salad.

Hellmann's mayonnaise was recommended for this recipe.

BLESS *us, O Lord, and these Thy gifts which we are about to receive* from Thy bounty through Christ our Lord. Amen.

SALMON MOUSSE

1	envelope unflavored gelatin	2	teaspoons lemon juice
¼	cup water	¼	teaspoon dill
1	cup sour cream	½	cup diced celery
½	cup mayonnaise	¼	cup diced onion
		1	(16 ounce) can salmon

Soften gelatin in water. Heat to dissolve gelatin; then cool. In large bowl, blend gelatin, sour cream, mayonnaise, lemon juice, and dill. Add celery and onion. Mix thoroughly. Drain and flake salmon and add to mixture. Place in 3-cup mold and chill to set.

Double recipe for 6-cup fish mold which makes a pretty presentation.
Yield: When served as an appetizer, fish mold yields 40 servings.

As a salad, 3-cup mold yields 6-8 servings.

ANGELS ON HORSEBACK

2	cups mayonnaise	2	pounds bacon, cut strips in half
1	tablespoon horseradish		
1	tablespoon Worcestershire sauce	2	tablespoons bacon grease or butter
2	teaspoons lemon juice	2	(8 ounce) cans water chestnuts, sliced
1	pound scallops		

Mix mayonnaise, horseradish, Worcestershire sauce, and lemon juice together. Add scallops and marinate 2 hours. Cook bacon slightly until curled but pliable. Sauté scallops in bacon grease or butter. Place one scallop, one slice water chestnut on bacon slice and wrap. Secure with toothpick. Broil 2-3 minutes fat side up. Serve hot.

BENNE SEED COCKTAILERS

2 cups flour
1 teaspoon salt
⅛ teaspoon cayenne pepper
¾ cup shortening or butter
Ice water
1 cup toasted benne seeds

Preheat oven to 300°. Toast benne seeds. Mix dry ingredients and cut in shortening. Add enough ice water to make the dough the consistency of pie crust. Add seeds. Roll out on lightly floured surface and cut with small round cutter. Place on cookie sheet and bake 15-20 minutes. Sprinkle with salt before removing from pan. Cool and store tightly covered.

Benne seeds are sesame seeds which can be found in grocery or health food stores.

HOT REUBEN DIP

*1 (8 ounce) package cream
cheese, softened*

½ cup sour cream

2 tablespoons ketchup

*½ pound deli corned beef,
finely chopped*

*1 cup sauerkraut, chopped,
rinsed, and drained*

1 cup shredded Swiss cheese

*2 tablespoons finely
chopped onion*

Snack rye bread or crackers

Preheat oven to 375°.
In a mixing bowl, beat cream
cheese, sour cream, and
ketchup until smooth. Stir in
the corned beef, sauerkraut,
Swiss cheese, and onion until
blended. Transfer to a greased
1-quart baking dish. Cover and
bake for 30 minutes. Uncover;
bake 5 minutes longer or
until bubbly. Serve warm
with bread or crackers.

Yield: 3 cups.

BLACK BEAN DIP

2	(11 ounce) cans black beans, rinsed	1	bunch green onions, chopped
1	(10 ounce) package frozen white corn	1	red pepper, chopped
		1	package dipping chips

DRESSING

¼	cup olive oil	¹⁄₁₆	teaspoon cumin
½	cup lemon juice		Garlic salt
1	cup mild prepared salsa		Salt and pepper to taste

Mix vegetables together in bowl. Mix dressing and pour over vegetables.
Use dipping chips to scoop dip.

    Yield: As an appetizer, 25-30 servings. As a salad, 10-12 servings.

Serve from a bowl as an appetizer or on a platter over lettuce as a salad.

HOT SHRIMP AND CRABMEAT DIP

1	(8 ounce) package cream cheese, cubed	⅓	teaspoon Worcestershire sauce
1	cup shredded sharp cheese	½	pound small cocktail shrimp, cooked and peeled
1	(10¾ ounce) can mushroom soup		
½	cup finely chopped onion	½	pound crabmeat
⅓	teaspoon hot pepper sauce		

Mix first 6 ingredients together and heat, stirring occasionally, until cheese
melts. Add shrimp and crabmeat. Blend until heated. Serve with crackers.

> ## BLESS
> *O Lord, this food to our use,
> and us to Thy service, and
> make us ever mindful of the needs of others. In
> Jesus' name. Amen.*

ASPARAGUS WITH WASABI-MAYONNAISE DIP

3	pounds thin medium asparagus, trimmed	2	teaspoons fresh lemon juice	
1	cup mayonnaise	2	teaspoons wasabi paste	
4	teaspoons soy sauce	½	teaspoon ground ginger	
1½	teaspoons sugar			

Blanch asparagus in 2 batches in a large saucepan of boiling salted water for 1 minute. Transfer to a colander and rinse under cold running water to stop cooking. Drain well and pat dry. Whisk together mayonnaise, soy sauce, sugar, lemon juice, wasabi paste, and ginger until sugar is dissolved. Serve asparagus with dip.

Yield: 6 servings.

Asparagus and dip may be prepared 1 day ahead, chill, and cover.

CARAMELIZED ONION DIP

1	teaspoon olive oil	⅓	cup low-fat mayonnaise	
1¾	cups chopped onion	⅓	cup nonfat sour cream	
1	garlic clove, minced	¼	teaspoon salt	
2	tablespoons cider vinegar	¼	cup plain nonfat yogurt	
4	tablespoons honey		Bagel chips	
¼	teaspoon white pepper			

Heat oil in large skillet over medium heat. Add onion and garlic. Cover and cook 8 minutes or until tender. Add vinegar, honey, and white pepper. Continue to stir. Bring to a boil over medium-high heat and cook uncovered for 10 minutes or until onion is deep golden and liquid evaporates, stirring occasionally. Combine the onion mixture with the next 4 ingredients in a bowl and stir well. Cover and chill. Serve with bagel chips.

CHEESE NUT LOAF

1 pound grated sharp cheese

1 cup chopped nut meats

1 handful parsley, chopped

1 small onion, diced

½ green pepper, seeded and diced

½ cup chili sauce

3 tablespoons mayonnaise

2 tablespoons steak or hot sauce

1 (8 ounce) package cream cheese

Onion juice

Salt

Pimentos and olives to decorate

Mix first 8 ingredients together and chill for several hours. Mold and cover with cream cheese seasoned with onion juice and salt. Decorate with pimentos and sliced olives. Serve with crackers.

Mrs. John T. Walker

HOT FETA ARTICHOKE DIP

1 (14 ounce) can artichoke hearts, drained and chopped
2 (4 ounce) packages crumbled Feta cheese
1 cup mayonnaise

½ cup shredded Parmesan cheese
1 (2 ounce) jar diced pimentos, drained
1 clove garlic, minced
Tomato and sliced green onion for garnish

Preheat oven to 350°. Mix first 6 ingredients together. Spoon into 9-inch pie plate or 3-cup shallow baking dish. Bake for 20-25 minutes or until lightly brown. Garnish with chopped tomato and sliced green onion. Serve with assorted crackers or pita triangles.

Yield: Makes 2 cups.

HOT CHEESE AND SUN-DRIED TOMATO DIP

1 onion, chopped
3 tablespoons butter
1 pound mushrooms, sliced
1½ cups mayonnaise
4 (3 ounce) packages cream cheese, softened
1 cup sour cream

2 tablespoons sun-dried tomatoes, minced and drained of oil
8 ounces shredded mozzarella cheese
8 ounces shredded Cheddar cheese
Salt and pepper to taste

Sauté onions in butter until edges are brown. Add mushrooms to pan. Let cool. Combine mayonnaise, cream cheese, and sour cream. Stir into onion mushroom mixture along with the sun-dried tomatoes. Stir in cheeses. Pour in a casserole dish, cover, and bake for 45 minutes. Serve with crackers.

Hellmann's mayonnaise was recommended for this recipe.

PUMPKIN DIP

1 (8 ounce) package cream cheese, softened	1 teaspoon cinnamon
1 (15 ounce) can pumpkin	½ teaspoon ground cloves

Mix all ingredients together and taste. Adjust spices if more are needed.

Yield: 3 cups.

Serve with apple slices or gingersnaps.

HUMMUS

2 (15 ounce) cans garbanzo beans	2 garlic cloves, minced
1 cup tahini	1 tablespoon olive oil
½ cup fresh lemon juice	1-2 teaspoons salt
	Parsley

Drain half of liquid from beans. Using a food processor or blender, process beans until smooth. Add remaining ingredients and process until very smooth and light. Chill for at least 3 hours. Garnish with parsley. Serve with pita bread or crackers.

Yield: 5 cups.

Tahini is made of crushed sesame seeds and can be found in most grocery stores and health food stores.

CORNED BEEF SPREAD

1 (12 ounce) can corned beef, crumbled	1 teaspoon minced onion
2 eggs, hard-boiled, finely chopped	3-4 tablespoons mayonnaise

Blend all ingredients well. Serve with crackers.

Yield: 2 cups.

NOTES

19

CHUTNEY CHEESE SPREAD

½   cup chutney
1   cup grated sharp Cheddar
     cheese
1   (3 ounce) package cream
     cheese, softened
3   green onions, minced
¼   teaspoon curry powder
¼   teaspoon ground ginger
¼   teaspoon salt
     Parsley

Remove fruit from chutney. Finely cut fruit and mix with chutney. In bowl, combine all ingredients. Chill about 6 hours or overnight. Serve with assorted crackers.

Yield: 40-50 servings.

This is a very nippy and tasty spread. It freezes well and is simple and quick to prepare.

Tip: Spread mixture into 2 saucer-sized bowls that have been lined with plastic wrap. Chill. After chilling, the spread can be transferred to small serving dishes.

FRUIT SALSA
AND CINNAMON CHIPS

2   kiwi, peeled and diced
2   golden delicious apples,
     peeled, cored, and diced
8   ounces raspberries
1   pound strawberries,
     halved
1   tablespoon white sugar
1   tablespoon brown sugar
3   tablespoons fruit
     preserves, any flavor
10 (10 inch) flour tortillas
     Butter flavored cooking
     spray
2   cups cinnamon sugar

In a large bowl, thoroughly mix kiwis, apples, raspberries, strawberries, sugars, and preserves. Cover and chill in the refrigerator at least 15 minutes.

Preheat oven to 350°.

Coat one side of each flour tortilla with butter flavored cooking spray. Cut into wedges and arrange in a single layer on a large baking sheet. Sprinkle wedges with desired amount of cinnamon sugar. Spray again with cooking spray.

Bake for 5-8 minutes. Repeat with any remaining tortilla wedges. Allow to cool approximately 15 minutes. Serve with chilled fruit mixture.

Yield: 10 servings.

CURRIED CANAPÉS

½ pound Cheddar cheese,
    grated
1 (10 ounce) jar green
    olives, chopped

1 bunch green onions,
    minced
1 cup mayonnaise
1 teaspoon curry

Mix all ingredients together and chill before serving. Serve with sesame toast rounds or shredded wheat crackers.

SHRIMP MOUSSE

1 (10¾ ounce) can tomato
    soup
½ can water
3 (3 ounce) packages cream
    cheese
2 tablespoons unflavored
    gelatin
½ cup water
1 cup mayonnaise

1½ cups finely chopped celery
1 cup finely chopped
    green pepper
1 medium finely chopped
    onion
1 (6 ounce) bag frozen,
    small cocktail shrimp;
    cooked and deveined

Bring soup and ½ can water to a boil. Add cream cheese. Cook until melted. Dissolve gelatin in ½ cup warm water and cool gelatin in refrigerator for 15 minutes. Add to soup mixture along with other ingredients and pour into lightly oiled 2-quart mold. Refrigerate until firm. Serve with crackers.

SHRIMP SEA ISLAND

HARBOR HOUSE BED AND BREAKFAST, GEORGETOWN, SC

5 pounds medium shrimp
5 Vidalia onions, thinly
    sliced
2 cups olive oil
1½ cups cider vinegar

1 (3½ ounce) bottle
    nonpareil capers and
    juice
½ cup sugar
¼ cup Worcestershire sauce
1 teaspoon hot pepper sauce
1 teaspoon salt

Cook, peel, and devein shrimp. Layer shrimp and onions in large dish. Mix all remaining ingredients. Pour over shrimp and marinate overnight.

Yield: 24-36 servings.

SHRIMP DIP

1 (6½ ounce) can shrimp or 1 cup fresh shrimp, boiled, and peeled	1 cup sour cream
1 (3 ounce) package cream cheese, softened	1 (.7 ounce) package dry Italian dressing mix

Drain shrimp and chop coarsely. Mix with other ingredients. Chill thoroughly before serving. Serve with crackers.

Yield: Makes 2 cups.

Low fat varieties may be substituted for cream cheese and sour cream.

This can be prepared ahead of time and refrigerated.

MEXICAN SHRIMP APPETIZER

½ pound fresh shrimp, cooked and shelled	1 (5¾ ounce) jar stuffed green olives, cut in half
⅓ cup oil	2 tablespoons minced parsley
Juice of 2 lemons	½ teaspoon oregano
Vinegar from jalapeño chilies (to taste)	Salt to taste
1 small onion, minced	Jalapeño chilies, chopped, to taste
2 medium tomatoes, peeled and chopped	

Marinate shrimp for 2 hours in mixture of oil, lemon juice, vinegar, and onion. Add tomatoes, olives, parsley, oregano, salt, and chopped jalapeños. Mix well. Allow to stand 2 hours longer before serving.

Can be prepared ahead.

SOUTHWEST APPETIZER CHEESECAKE

⅔ cup crushed tortilla chips	½ cup sour cream
2 tablespoons butter, melted	1 (8 ounce) can prepared
1 cup cottage cheese	jalapeño-Cheddar dip
3 (8 ounce) packages cream cheese	½ cup chopped green onions
4 eggs	¼ cup sliced, pitted ripe olives
10 ounces shredded sharp Cheddar cheese	1 cup chopped tomatoes
1 (4 ounce) can chopped green chilies, drained	Salsa

Preheat oven to 325°. Mix chips and butter together. Press into bottom of 9-inch springform pan. Bake for 15 minutes. Place cottage cheese in blender and mix until smooth. In a large bowl, mix cottage cheese and cream cheese until well blended. Add eggs, one at a time, mixing well after each egg. Spoon in Cheddar cheese and green chilies. Pour mixture over baked chips and bake for 1 hour. Mix together sour cream and jalapeño-Cheddar dip. Pour over hot cheesecake and return to oven. Bake an additional 10 minutes; remove and let cool. Loosen cheesecake from pan and cool completely. Refrigerate until ready to serve. Top with tomatoes, green onions, and olives. Cut as you would cheesecake and serve with salsa.

Yield: 9-12 servings.

GIVE *us grateful hearts, our Father, for all Thy mercies, and make us mindful of the needs of others. Blessed are you, O Lord God, King of the Universe, for You give us food to sustain our lives and make our hearts glad, through Jesus Christ our Lord. Amen.*

MELTED CHEDDAR AND CUMIN CANAPÉS

Fresh white bread

Toast rounds made from bread, using either a cookie cutter or wine glass. Toast in oven on 1 side.

FILLING

¾ cup grated sharp Cheddar cheese	2 tablespoons mayonnaise
½ cup ripe, pitted black olives, coarsely chopped	¼ teaspoon cumin
	⅛ teaspoon ground ginger
	¼ teaspoon cayenne pepper
¼ cup chopped shallots	¼ teaspoon salt (optional)

Thoroughly combine all ingredients and spread on the untoasted side of the bread rounds. Broil for 1-2 minutes until cheese starts to melt. Best served hot.

Yield: 4 servings.

HOT MACADAMIA SPREAD

1 (8 ounce) package cream cheese, softened	1 green onion, chopped
2 tablespoons milk	½ teaspoon garlic salt
½ cup sour cream	¼ teaspoon pepper
2 teaspoons prepared horseradish	½ cup chopped macadamia nuts or blanched almonds
¼ cup finely chopped green pepper	2 teaspoons butter
	Assorted crackers

Preheat oven to 350°. In a mixing bowl, beat cream cheese and milk until smooth. Stir in sour cream, horseradish, green pepper, onion, garlic salt, and pepper. Spoon into an ungreased shallow 2-cup baking dish; set aside. In a skillet, sauté the nuts in butter for 3-4 minutes or until lightly browned. Sprinkle over the cream cheese mixture. Bake uncovered for 20 minutes. Serve with crackers.

Yield: 6-8 servings.

Roasted Bell Pepper and Artichoke Pizza

1	teaspoon olive oil	¼	teaspoon freshly ground black pepper
2	cloves garlic, minced, divided	1	(9 ounce) package frozen artichoke hearts, thawed and drained
1	red bell pepper, roasted, peeled, seeded, and cut into strips	1	ready-made pizza crust (1 pound), plain or cheese flavored
1	orange bell pepper, roasted, peeled, seeded, and cut into strips	½	cup feta cheese, crumbled
¼	cup reduced fat mayonnaise	1	teaspoon chopped fresh thyme
⅛	teaspoon crushed red pepper		

Preheat oven to 450°. Heat oil in a nonstick skillet over medium-high heat. Sauté 1 clove garlic for 1 minute. Stir in bell peppers. Set aside. Place remaining garlic, mayonnaise, red pepper, black pepper, and artichoke hearts in a food processor. Process until finely chopped. Place pizza crust on a greased baking sheet or pizza stone. Spread artichoke over crust, leaving a ½-inch border. Top with bell pepper mixture. Sprinkle with feta and thyme. Bake 14 minutes or until crust is crisp. Slice and serve.

Yield: 8 servings.

Feta cheese will not melt.

SO I *commend the enjoyment of life because nothing is better for a man under the sun than to eat and drink and be glad. Then joy will accompany him in his work all the days of the life God has given him under the sun. Ecclesiastes 8:15*

PESTO, HAM AND CHEESE ROLLUPS

1 tube crescent roll dough

4 tablespoons pesto

4 paper-thin slices of luncheon ham

4 slices paper-thin Swiss cheese

Unroll dough and press 2 squares together end-to-end. Press all perforations together. Spread with approximately 2 tablespoons of pesto, maybe less. Place 2 slices of ham on rectangle. Do the same with the cheese. From one of the short sides, roll tightly like a jelly roll to the center. Repeat with other short side until the two rolls meet in the center. Repeat the above and make a second roll. Wrap in plastic wrap and chill for 2 hours or overnight. This can be done the day before serving.

To bake, preheat oven to 375°. Slice the rolls ⅜-inch thick and place cut-side down on a lightly greased cookie sheet. Bake for 10-12 minutes. Serve warm.

CHORIZO TAQUITOS WITH DIP

½	cup salsa	2	cups shredded mild Cheddar cheese
½	cup sour cream		
½	pound chorizo sausage	12	soft taco-size flour tortillas

Preheat oven to 400°. Line 2 cookie sheets with foil.

For dip, mix together salsa and sour cream. Set aside.

Brown the chorizo over medium heat for 6 minutes or until browned, stirring occasionally. Lay one tortilla flat in front of you. Spoon ¼ cup of chorizo down the middle. Top with 1½ tablespoons cheese. Roll up, using a toothpick to hold together. Place seam-side down on cookie sheet. Repeat with all tortillas. Bake taquitos for 10 minutes or until slightly crisp. Remove toothpicks. Slice taquitos in half. Serve warm with salsa-sour cream dip.

Yield: 24 servings.

STUFFED GRAPE LEAVES

2	pounds very lean ground beef or lamb	1	(8 ounce) jar grape leaves (if you can get them loose in brine, they are better)
2	cups cooked long-grain rice		
2	teaspoons salt	1	small piece of lamb with round bone in
1	teaspoon allspice		
1	clove garlic, minced	½	cup lemon juice
¼	cup butter, melted		

Combine all the ingredients except grape leaves, lamb and lemon juice. Rinse grape leaves several times and remove stem. To roll, place grape leaf top-side down, working with the underside of the leaf. Put about 1 heaping tablespoon of mixture on the leaf, forming it into a log ½-inch by 2½-inches. Begin rolling from the wide, stem end of the leaf; after first roll, turn in left and right sides of leaf. Finish by rolling to the end of the leaf. Put a few leaves and a small piece of lamb in the bottom of a heavy pot. Layer stuffed grape leaves in pot, adding rows as needed. Cover with a few grape leaves. Add water to the top of the stuffed grape leaves. Pour in lemon juice. Place a heavy plate on top and bring to a boil. Lower heat and simmer for 1 hour. Remove with tongs. Water should be almost gone. Serve warm or cold.

Yield: 24-30 servings.

These could be served as an appetizer or a main course.

SAUSAGE WONTONS

1   pound sausage, crumbled
    and cooked
1   cup Ranch dressing
1½ cups grated sharp cheese
1½ cups grated Monterey Jack
    cheese
1   (4 ounce) can chopped
    black olives
1   (2 ounce) jar chopped
    pimentos
1   bunch green onions,
    including the tops,
    chopped
1   package wonton wrappers

Preheat oven to 350°. Mix all ingredients except wonton wrappers. Place wonton wrapper in mini-muffin pan. Bake for 3 minutes or until just lightly brown. Remove from oven. Fill wonton with sausage mixture. Bake 5-7 minutes.

Yield: 10-12 servings.

The jalapeño variety of Monterey Jack cheese may be used if a spicier flavor is desired.

PARTY HAM ROLLS

1   cup butter, softened
3   tablespoons poppy seeds
1   tablespoon Worcestershire
    sauce
3   tablespoons Dijon mustard
1   medium onion, grated
2   (12 ounce) packages party
    rolls
½   pound Swiss cheese,
    grated
½   pound or more chipped
    ham

Preheat oven to 400°. Mix first 5 ingredients. Slice entire pan of rolls at one time. Spread mix on both sides. Put ham on bottom half. Sprinkle with cheese and place other half on top. Wrap in foil and bake 10-15 minutes. Let cool before slicing rolls apart.

Yield: 40 servings.

If rolls have been refrigerated, they will take longer to heat.

Grey Poupon Dijon Mustard and Pepperidge Farm Party Rolls were recommended for this recipe.

GOOD PIMENTO CHEESE

1 (3 ounce) package cream cheese, softened

1 cup grated sharp Cheddar cheese

1 cup grated Monterey Jack cheese

½ cup mayonnaise

⅛ teaspoon garlic powder

⅛ teaspoon black pepper

¼ teaspoon salt

1 teaspoon grated onion

2 tbsp pimiento

Using electric mixer, beat cream cheese until smooth and fluffy. Add remaining ingredients and beat until well blended.

Great on crackers or as a sandwich filling.

TEX-MEX EGG ROLLS WITH DIPPING SAUCE

1	(5 ounce) package Spanish rice mix
1	teaspoon salt
1	pound hot pork sausage
1	(15 ounce) can black beans, rinsed and drained
1	(14½ ounce) can diced petite tomatoes with mild green chilies, not drained
2	cups shredded Monterey Jack cheese
6	green onions, finely chopped
1	(1¼ ounce) package taco seasoning
28	egg roll wrappers
1	large egg, lightly beaten
4	cups peanut oil
	Fresh cilantro sprigs for garnish

Cook rice according to package directions with 1 teaspoon salt. Cool completely. Cook sausage in a skillet over medium heat, stirring until it crumbles and is no longer pink; drain well. Let cool. Stir together rice, sausage, black beans, tomatoes with chilies, cheese, onions, and taco seasoning in a large bowl. Spoon about ⅓ cup rice mixture in center of each egg roll wrapper. Fold top corner of wrapper over filling, tucking tip of corner under filling; fold left and right corners over filling. Lightly brush remaining corner with egg; tightly roll filled end toward the remaining corner, and gently press to seal. Pour oil into heavy Dutch oven; heat to 375°. Fry egg rolls in batches, 2-3 minutes or until golden. Drain on wire rack over paper towels. Serve with cilantro dipping sauce. Garnish, if desired.

Yield: 28 servings.

CREAMY CILANTRO DIPPING SAUCE

2	(10 ounce) cans diced tomatoes with lime juice and cilantro
1	(8 ounce) package cream cheese, softened
2	cups fresh cilantro (about 1 bunch)
1	cup sour cream
3	garlic cloves, minced

Process diced tomatoes and all other ingredients in a food processor until smooth. Garnish, if desired.

Yield: Makes 3 cups.

For a beautiful presentation, cut top from large red bell pepper, reserving top; remove and discard seeds and membrane, leaving pepper intact. Arrange bell pepper on a serving plate and fill with sauce.

Bruschetta with Tomato, Basil, and Mozzarella

1	pound Roma tomatoes, peeled and seeded	2	tablespoons extra virgin olive oil
2	medium garlic cloves, minced	½	teaspoon balsamic vinegar
3	tablespoons finely chopped fresh basil	½	teaspoon salt
1	tablespoon finely chopped Italian parsley	½	teaspoon coarse black pepper
		¼	pound fresh mozzarella cheese, grated

To make relish: Dice tomatoes into ½-inch pieces; drain over a bowl for ½ hour to remove excess liquid. Combine all relish ingredients in a non-aluminum bowl. Stir well and taste for seasoning. Mix ahead of time and refrigerate.

Bread
1 medium baguette, sourdough or Italian bread

Cut bread into ½-inch slices and lightly toast. Top with the relish and put under broiler for approximately 2 minutes.

Plantation Tours Spiced Tea

48	cups water, divided	9	cups orange juice without pulp
1	cup loose tea or 8 tea bags		
6	cups sugar	6	tablespoons lemon juice
1	tablespoon whole cloves		

Boil 24 cups of water with tea. Set aside to steep for 10 minutes. To the second 24 cups of water add sugar and cloves. Heat to make sugar syrup or until sugar dissolves. Strain tea. Mix tea and sugar syrup with orange juice and lemon juice.

Yield: 85 servings.

Served at the Winyah Indigo Society Hall during Plantation Tours Weekend!

CITRUS WHIP

½ cup orange juice
¼ cup lemon juice
½ teaspoon grated lemon rind
1 cup lemon sherbet
10 ice cubes
2-4 tablespoons dry sherry (optional)

Combine first 3 ingredients in blender. Process on BLEND for 5 seconds. Add sherbet and ice cubes, process on BLEND for 1 minute until frothy. Process again while adding sherry. Serve in parfait or wine glasses immediately.

Yield: 4 servings.

This is very mild and good for serving ladies.

GEORGETOWN CENTER PUNCH

3 dozen lemons

2 pounds sugar

¹/₁₆ teaspoon salt

2 quarts water

3 (46 ounce) cans sweetened orange juice

3 (46 ounce) cans sweetened grapefruit juice

3 (46 ounce) cans sweetened pineapple juice

6 (1 liter) bottles ginger ale

Squeeze lemons. To the lemon juice add sugar, salt, and water. Boil 20 minutes. Cool. Put lemon syrup in jars. Prepare to serve ⅓ of recipe at a time by mixing one large can each of orange, grapefruit, and pineapple juice with 1 quart lemon syrup. Pour over ice in punch bowl and add 2 liters ginger ale.

Yield: 60 servings.

OPEN HOUSE PUNCH

8	cups unsweetened tea, chilled	4	cups lemonade, chilled
8	cups cranberry juice, chilled	2	(2 liter) bottles ginger ale, chilled
8	cups orange juice, chilled		

Mix ingredients together. Add ginger ale just before serving.

Yield: 60 servings.

SUMMER PUNCH

1	(12 ounce) can frozen lemonade concentrate	5	pints (or 10 cups) pineapple sherbet
1	(6 ounce) can frozen orange juice concentrate	1	(½ gallon) carton vanilla ice cream
8	cups water	1	(1 liter) bottle ginger ale

Mix juices and water. Add sherbet, ice cream, and ginger ale just before serving.

Yield: 30 servings.

MRS. COLES PUNCH

1	(6 ounce) can frozen lemonade or limeade concentrate	1½	cups pineapple juice
		10	ounces water
1½	cups apricot nectar	2	cups ginger ale

Combine first 4 ingredients. Stir well. Just before serving add the ginger ale. Rum can be added for an extra kick.

Yield: 12 servings.

BRUNCH PUNCH

1	gallon apple juice	8-16	ounces grenadine or cherry juice for color
1	gallon orange juice		
1	gallon pineapple juice	1-2	bottles of champagne OR 1 additional liter of ginger ale
1	(1 liter) bottle ginger ale		

Prepare with enough time to chill punch or prepare with ingredients that have already been chilled. Mix apple, orange, pineapple juices, and ginger ale together. Add grenadine or cherry juice to achieve desired color. This can be done in advance or just prior to serving. Chill. Add champagne just before serving. Serve chilled in fancy glasses or flutes.

Yield: 100 servings.

CRIMSON CRANBERRY PUNCH

½	cup fresh or frozen cranberries	2	(12 ounce) cans frozen cranberry juice concentrate, thawed
	Nonstick cooking spray		
4	cups cold water	4	(12 ounce) cans diet lemon-lime soda, chilled
1	(48 ounce) bottle white grape juice, chilled		
		3	orange slices
		3	lemon slices

Place the cranberries in a 4½ cup ring mold coated with nonstick cooking spray. Slowly pour a small amount of cold water into the mold to barely cover berries; freeze until solid. Add remaining water; freeze until solid. Just prior to serving, combine the grape juice and cranberry juice concentrate in a large punch bowl; stir in soda. Unmold ice ring; place fruit side up in punch bowl. Add orange and lemon slices.

Yield: 25 servings.

BLOODY MARY PUNCH

1 (46 ounce) can vegetable juice or tomato juice, chilled

¾ cup vodka, chilled

1 teaspoon freshly ground pepper

3 tablespoons lime juice

1-2 tablespoons hot sauce, optional

2 tablespoons Worcestershire sauce

1 teaspoon seafood seasoning

Celery sticks (optional)

Combine all ingredients except celery in a punch bowl or a pitcher. Serve over ice in glasses. Serve with celery.

Yield: 8 servings.

DECORATIVE ICE MOLDS OR RINGS

These are beautiful additions to the punch. Fill the mold about ⅓ full of water or fruit juice and freeze. Add lemon, lime, orange slices, cherries, strawberries, grape clusters, and/or fresh mint. Cover with cold water or juice and freeze. Repeat the process making sure that each layer is completely surrounded by clear ice.

PARTY PUNCH

3	cups water	1½	cups canned frozen orange juice concentrate
1	cup sugar	1½	cups canned frozen lemonade concentrate
1	(6 ounce) package dry gelatin, any color	1	cup bottled lemon juice
½	cup canned unsweetened pineapple juice	1	(2 liter) bottle ginger ale, chilled

In a saucepan, heat water and sugar, stirring until sugar is dissolved. Remove from heat. Add gelatin and continue to stir until gelatin is completely dissolved. Add juices, one at a time, blending well. Pour immediately into several small plastic containers, cover, and freeze. This punch concentrate can be frozen for up to three months. Prior to serving, break up mixture with a fork and put chunks into a punchbowl. Pour ginger ale over this. Allow time before serving for punch to defrost to a cold liquid.

Yield: 18 servings.

SOUTHERN SWEET TEA
The "Important Beverage" of the South

The making of sweet tea cannot be taken lightly. Certain points must be remembered. First: the water should be clear and not hard. Second: the water should just come to a boil; never allow boiling water to touch the tea. Third: do not allow the tea to brew too long or it will become bitter. Fourth: store in a cool place, but not in the refrigerator where it will become cloudy.

4	regular-size tea bags	4	minutes to steep
4	cups cool water	4	teaspoons or tablespoons sugar, to taste
4	minutes in microwave on high		

Make tea and pour cooled tea over lots of ice and enjoy!

Yield: 4 servings.

PEACH SMOOTHIE

1	cup raspberries	1	teaspoon vanilla extract
1	cup ice cubes	1	(12 ounce) can peach nectar, chilled
1	cup sliced peaches		
2	tablespoons sugar	1	cup seltzer water, chilled Fresh mint springs (optional)

Process raspberries in blender until smooth. Strain and discard seeds. Combine raspberry purée and next 5 ingredients in blender. Blend until smooth. Pour into a pitcher, stir in seltzer. Garnish with mint. Serve immediately.

Yield: 5 servings.

PINEAPPLE SMOOTHIES

1½	cups sweetened pineapple juice	2	cups ice cubes
1	cup 1% buttermilk	2	(8 ounce) cans sweetened crushed pineapple

Combine all ingredients in a blender or food processor; cover and process until smooth. Pour into glasses. Serve immediately.

Yield: 6 servings.

SPICED PEAR AND APPLE CIDER

6	cups apple cider	3	whole cinnamon sticks
6	cups pear nectar	¼	teaspoon ground nutmeg
1	(2 inch) piece peeled fresh ginger, cut into thin rounds	¼	teaspoon cinnamon
		10	whole cloves

In a saucepan, stir together apple cider and pear nectar. Add remaining ingredients; bring to a boil. Reduce heat; simmer, stirring 20 to 25 minutes. Serve hot.

Yield: 11 cups.

ICE RING WREATH

4 cups cold water, divided

Nonstick cooking spray

3 large limes

1 (12 ounce) package fresh cranberries

Pour 1 cup water into a 4½ cup ring mold that is lightly coated with nonstick cooking spray. Peel limes, keeping peel in large pieces. Using miniature tree or leaf cookie cutters, cut trees or leaves from the peel. Place shapes upside down on top of ring mold. Place cranberries between tree or leaf shapes. Rearrange if necessary before freezing. Freeze until solid.

Gently add remaining water; freeze. To use: wrap bottom of solidly frozen mold in a warm towel until loosened or dip mold in pan of warm water. Float ice ring, fruit side up, in cold punch.

Freeze strawberries, pitted cherries, raspberries, grapes or mint in ice cube trays using some of the punch or fruit drink as the liquid. Float these in the punch or in individual cups.

COLD RUSSIAN TEA

6 lemons

6 oranges

1 quart boiling water

2 pounds sugar

1 pint strong tea

2 ounces sherry wine

Remove juices from fruit. Pour boiling water over the rinds. Drain, add sugar, boil 5 minutes and cool. Add juices, tea, and wine. Serve in glasses of crushed ice, garnished with mint.

Yield: 8 servings.

Margaret D. Richardson

RED SANGRÍA

2	lemons	8	cups dry red wine
2	oranges	1	cup apricot brandy
6	tablespoons sugar	2	(1 liter) bottles club soda
6	tablespoons lemon juice		Ice

Wash oranges and lemons; slice paper thin with seeds removed. Put sugar, lemon juice, and fruit into a tall pitcher. Allow to stand 1 hour. Add wine and brandy; let stand another 30 minutes to blend all flavors. When ready to serve, add both bottles of club soda and plenty of ice and stir. When pouring, include some fruit in each glass.

Yield: 18-25 servings.

EVER READY DAIQUIRIS

2	(6 ounce) cans frozen lemonade concentrate	2	(46 ounce) cans pineapple juice
2	(6 ounce) cans frozen limeade concentrate	4	cups rum

Combine all ingredients. Place in freezer overnight. These will not completely freeze. They will be slushy with slivers of ice.

Yield: 34 servings.

Great beach drink! If they do freeze, just let them sit out for a while.

PEACH FUZZ BUZZES

4	medium peaches, peeled, cut into pieces	10	ounces vodka
1	(6 ounce) can frozen pink lemonade concentrate	1	cup of ice

Place all ingredients in blender with ice. Blend until thick and smooth. Add ice as needed.

Yield: 4 servings.

STRAWBERRY MARGARITA

1	(8 ounce) package frozen strawberries, partially thawed	⅓	cup powdered sugar
5	cups ice	3	tablespoons Grand Marnier
½	cup tequila		Lime juice
½	cup thawed limeade concentrate		Red sugar crystals
			Garnishes: lime slices, fresh strawberries

Process first 6 ingredients in a blender until smooth. Dip margarita glass rims in lime juice; dip rims in red sugar crystals, coating well. Pour margarita mixture into glasses. Serve immediately. Garnish if desired.

Yield: 5 servings.

RED ROOSTER

1	(12 ounce) can frozen lemonade concentrate	1	(32 ounce) bottle cranberry juice
1	(12 ounce) can frozen limeade concentrate	4	cups vodka
		1	(6 ounce) can frozen limeade concentrate

Prepare lemonade and limeade according to package directions. Mix together; add cranberry juice and vodka. Stir in frozen limeade. Serve immediately.

Yield: 20 servings.

ORANGE LIQUEUR REFRESHER

2	cups ice cubes	¼	cup orange juice
¼	cup vodka		Orange slices for garnish, optional
2	tablespoons orange liqueur		

Combine first 4 ingredients in a martini shaker. Cover with lid, and shake until thoroughly chilled. Remove lid, and strain into a chilled martini glass. Serve immediately. Garnish if desired with orange slice.

Yield: 1 serving.

MINT JULEP MARTINI

¼ cup bourbon

¼ cup orange liqueur

1 teaspoon vanilla extract

1 teaspoon clear crème de menthe

6 ice cubes

Garnishes: fresh mint sprig, orange rind curl

Combine first 5 ingredients in a martini shaker. Cover with lid, and shake until thoroughly chilled. Remove lid, and strain into a chilled martini glass. Serve immediately. Garnish, if desired.

Yield: 2 servings.

DADDY'S FAVORITE BRANDY ALEXANDER

1 (1½ gallon) carton coffee ice cream OR 1 (1½ gallon) carton vanilla ice cream plus

1 tablespoon instant coffee

½ cup brandy

¼ cup chocolate liqueur or coffee liqueur

Blend in large blender for 1 minute or until smooth.

Yield: 4 cups.

PINK POINSETTIA

6	ounces champagne, chilled	Cranberry juice, chilled
3	ounces triple sec	

Divide the champagne and triple sec between two champagne glasses. Add a splash of cranberry juice and stir gently.

Yield: 2 servings.

This is a wonderful, light Christmas drink.

JOEL ROBERTS POINSETT

He was born in Charleston, South Carolina, on March 2, 1779. In 1833 he married Mary Izard Pringle. Though he had an outstanding career as a United States Congressman and Ambassador to Mexico, he is best known for his discovery of a beautiful shrub with large red flowers growing near a road in Mexico in 1826. He took cuttings from the plant and brought them back to his greenhouse in South Carolina. William Prescott, historian and horticulturist, named the plant POINSETTIA in honor of Joel Poinsett's discovery. Poinsett also spearheaded what is now known as the Smithsonian Institution. He died at age 72 near what is now Statesburg, South Carolina on December 12, 1851, and is interred in the Church of the Holy Cross Episcopal Cemetery in Statesburg, South Carolina.

CHRISTMAS CAPPUCCINO

1	cup powdered nondairy creamer	½	teaspoon ground cinnamon
1	cup powdered chocolate drink mix	¼	teaspoon ground nutmeg
⅔	cup instant coffee granules		Boiling water
½	cup sugar		Ice cream, if desired
			Whipped topping, if desired

Mix dry ingredients together. Store in airtight container. To serve, combine 1 tablespoon plus 1 teaspoon dry mix into a cup. Add 1 cup boiling water. Top with ice cream or whipped topping if desired.

WHEN *they had finished eating, Jesus said to Simon Peter, "Son of John, do you truly love me more than these?" "Yes, Lord," he said "you know that I love you." Jesus said, "Feed my sheep." John 21: 15*

COFFEE PUNCH

8	cups strong, cold coffee	1	quart vanilla ice cream
1	quart cold milk	1	cup heavy cream, whipped
2½	teaspoons vanilla extract		Ground nutmeg, to taste
½	cup granulated sugar		

In a large bowl or pitcher, combine coffee, milk, vanilla extract, and sugar. Stir until sugar is dissolved. Chill thoroughly. To serve: place ice cream in punch bowl and pour coffee mixture on top. Top with whipped cream and sprinkle with nutmeg.

Yield: 12 cups.

CHOCOLATE PUNCH

2	(½ gallon) cartons chocolate ice cream, divided	1½	cups chocolate syrup Milk
		1	(1 liter) ginger ale, or more

Place ½ gallon ice cream in a gallon glass jar. Add chocolate syrup. Fill jar with milk. Refrigerate 8-10 hours.

To serve, put second ½ gallon ice cream in a punch bowl and pour milk mixture over it. Add 2 cups ginger ale for each gallon of punch.

Yield: Each gallon glass jar makes about 20 6-ounce cups.

A decanter of rum may be placed on the table; a delicious addition. Assume that each person will have 3-4 cups of punch — and they will!!

HOT SPICED TEA

1 teaspoon whole cloves
1 small piece stick cinnamon
3 quarts water
3 tablespoons tea
1 cup sugar
4 oranges, squeezed
2 lemons, squeezed

Tie spices loosely in a cloth bag. Bring water to a boil. Add tea tied loosely in a cloth bag. Steep 5 minutes. Remove bags. Add sugar and fruit juices; stir until sugar is melted. Add more sugar if needed.

Yield: 25 servings.

Cleo Kaminski

NOTES

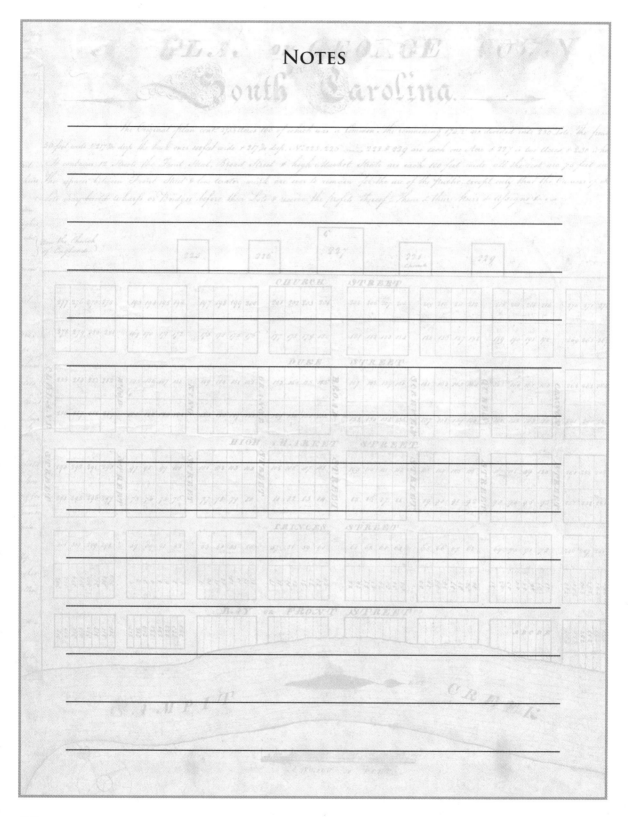

BREADS & BRUNCH

THE ELEAZER WATERMAN HOUSE

Title: Georgetown Spring

Artist: Joseph Cave

The Eleazer Waterman House is located on Highmarket Street in Georgetown. Albert Simons, a noted Charleston architect, wrote, "This house has all the signs of having been built sometime between the middle of the 18th century and the Revolution." It is a two and one-half story frame house with clapboard siding in the Charleston style. Unlike most houses of this period, the charming piazza was built at the time of construction. It originally extended around the street facade with what is now the center window being the front door.

It is not until 1854, however, that a legal record of this property could be found. In 1854, it was sold by Eleazer Waterman and some members of his family. Mr. Waterman was an influential member of the merchant class that had developed in Georgetown, and in 1862 he served as Ordinary (an official who has immediate jurisdiction). In his HISTORY OF GEORGETOWN COUNTY, George Rogers wrote, "On April 22, 1862, F. S. Parker ordered Eleazer Waterman, Ordinary, to pack his records in one large case and one box and have them sent to the Clerk of Court in Chesterfield District." The records were removed to Chesterfield Court House. Consequently, our Georgetown records were lost when General William T. Sherman's army burned the Chesterfield Courthouse.

Most of the interior woodwork in the house is original. Two mantels, one candlelight and one paneled, have been described as the finest in the Waccamaw region and of museum quality. The doors have raised panels and the window lights are nine-over-nine.

Mrs. Nathan Kaminski, current owner, has carefully preserved the prominent architectural features of this handsome dwelling.

BAKED CHEESE BLINTZ
A RECIPE FROM THE RECTORY

½	cup butter	1¼	cups flour
½	cup sugar	1	teaspoon baking powder
2	eggs	½	teaspoon salt
¾	cup milk		

FILLING

1	pound ricotta cheese	1	tablespoon sugar
2	tablespoons butter, melted		Cinnamon
1	egg, beaten		

Preheat oven to 350°. Grease 9x9-inch pan. Cream butter and sugar. Add eggs, milk, flour, baking powder, and salt. Mix until smooth. Combine cheese, melted butter, egg, sugar, and cinnamon for filling. Pour half of batter into pan. Cover with filling mixture. Then cover with remaining batter. Bake 1 hour.

Yield: 9 squares.
This is easily doubled, using a 9x13-inch pan.

Yield: 18 servings.
Serve sour cream and strawberries in separate bowls as optional toppings.

SOUR CREAM CAKE

½	cup butter	1	teaspoon baking soda
1	cup sugar	¼	teaspoon salt
2	eggs	1	cup sour cream
2	cups flour	1	teaspoon vanilla extract
1	teaspoon baking powder		

TOPPING

½	cup sugar	½	cup chopped nuts
1	teaspoon cinnamon		

Preheat oven to 350°. Grease tube or Bundt pan. Cream butter and sugar. Add eggs 1 at a time, beating well after each. Sift dry ingredients together and add alternately to batter with sour cream and vanilla extract. Pour ½ of batter into tube or Bundt pan. Sprinkle a little more than ½ of nut mixture on top. Add remaining batter and sprinkle with rest of nut mixture. Bake for 45 minutes.

Yield: 16 servings.
If you are a chocolate lover, add 1 cup of semi-sweet chocolate chips to topping mix.

SLEEP OVER COFFEE CAKE

CAKE

2	cups flour		2	tablespoons dry milk
1	cup sugar		1	tablespoon cinnamon
1	cup buttermilk		1	teaspoon baking soda
⅔	cup butter		1	teaspoon baking powder
½	cup brown sugar		½	teaspoon salt
2	large eggs			

COFFEE CAKE TOPPING

½	cup brown sugar		½	teaspoon nutmeg
½	cup chopped nuts		¼	cup melted butter

NIGHT BEFORE. Grease and flour 9x13-inch pan. Mix cake ingredients at low speed for 4 minutes. In a separate bowl, prepare coffee cake topping by mixing brown sugar, chopped nuts, and nutmeg together. Spread batter in pan and sprinkle coffee cake topping mixture over the top. Cover and refrigerate overnight.

NEXT AM. Preheat oven to 350°. Drizzle melted butter on top of cake and bake 30 minutes or more. Cool 15 minutes before serving.

Yield: 12-16 servings.

I WILL *make a covenant of peace with them and rid the land of wild beasts so that they may live in the desert and sleep in the forests in safety. I will bless them and the places surrounding my hill. I will send down showers in season; there will be showers of blessing. The trees of the field will yield their fruit; and the ground will yield its crops; the people will be secure in their land. They will know that I am the Lord. Ezekiel 34:25-27*

APRICOT COFFEE CAKE

3¼	cups biscuit baking mix	2	eggs
¾	cup sugar	1	cup milk
⅛	teaspoon ground cardamom	⅔	cup sour cream
		1	tablespoon butter, melted

Preheat oven to 350°. In a large bowl, combine the biscuit mix, sugar, and cardamom. Combine the eggs, milk, sour cream, and butter; stir into dry ingredients just until moistened. Prepare Pecan Topping. (Recipe below).

Spread a third of the batter into a 10-inch tube or Bundt pan coated with nonstick cooking spray. Spread with half of the pecan topping. Repeat layers. Top with the remaining batter.

Bake 40-45 minutes or until a toothpick comes out clean. Cool for 15 minutes; remove from pan to a wire rack.

PECAN TOPPING

1	(10 ounce) jar 100% apricot spreadable fruit, divided	⅓	cup sugar
		4	teaspoons ground cinnamon
¾	cup chopped pecans		

Place 3 tablespoons spreadable fruit in a small microwave-safe bowl; cover and refrigerate. In another bowl, combine the pecans, sugar, cinnamon, and remaining spreadable fruit; set aside.

In a microwave, warm the reserved spreadable fruit; brush over warm cake. Cool completely.

Yield: 16 servings.

FOR *the bread of God is He who comes down from heaven and gives life to the world. John 6:33*

CRAN-APPLE RING

1	(¼ ounce) package active dry yeast	2¾-3¼	cups all-purpose flour
¼	cup warm water (110° to 115°)	1¼	cups thinly sliced peeled apples
½	cup warm milk (110° to 115°)	1¼	cups dried cranberries
1	egg	¾	cup chopped walnuts, toasted
2	tablespoons butter, softened	1½	teaspoons ground cinnamon
1	tablespoon grated orange peel	1	egg white
1	teaspoon salt	1	tablespoon water
3	tablespoons + ½ cup sugar	½	cup powdered sugar
		1	tablespoon orange juice
			Vegetable cooking spray

Preheat oven to 375°. In a mixing bowl, dissolve yeast in warm water. Add milk, egg, butter, orange peel, salt, 3 tablespoons sugar, and 1 cup flour; beat until smooth. Stir in enough remaining flour to form a soft dough. Knead until smooth and elastic, about 6-8 minutes. Place in a bowl coated with nonstick cooking spray; turn once to coat. Cover and let rise in a warm place for 1 hour. In a separate bowl, toss the fruit, walnuts, cinnamon, and ½ cup sugar; set aside. Punch dough down; turn onto a lightly floured surface. Roll into a 20x10-inch rectangle. Combine egg white and water; chill 3 tablespoons of mixture. Brush remaining mixture over dough. Spoon fruit mixture within 1 inch of edges. Roll up tightly jelly-roll style, starting with a long side; seal ends.

Place seam side down in a 15x10x1-inch baking pan coated with nonstick cooking spray; pinch ends to form a ring. With scissors, cut from outside edge ⅔ of the way toward center of ring at 1-inch intervals. Separate strips slightly; twist so filling shows. Cover and let rise until doubled, about 40 minutes. Brush with reserved egg white mixture. Bake for 20-25 minutes or until golden brown (cover loosely with foil during the last 10 minutes). Remove to a wire rack to cool. Combine powdered sugar and orange juice; drizzle over ring.

Yield: 16 servings.

Mrs. Bull's Banana Nut Bread

½ cup butter, softened	2 cups flour
1 cup sugar	½ teaspoon soda
2 eggs	½ teaspoon baking powder
3 large ripe bananas, mashed	1 teaspoon salt
½ cup chopped nuts	1 teaspoon vanilla extract

Preheat oven to 350°. Grease 9½ x 5¼-inch loaf pan. Cream butter and sugar. Add eggs, one at a time, and beat well. Add bananas and nuts. Add flour, sifted with soda, baking powder, and salt. Add vanilla extract. Bake in loaf pan for 1 hour or until done.

This bread is served at afternoon tea. The tea, which has now become a fixed event on each tour day, had its beginning through the kindness of Miss Charlotte Pyatt. She opened Richmond Lodge in 1957 and decided to serve tea and homemade cookies to the weary tourists at the end of the day. This she did for a number of years.

MRS. EMILY BULL

Old-Fashioned Pumpkin Bread

1⅔ cups flour	1⅓ cups sugar
¼ teaspoon baking powder	1 teaspoon vanilla extract
1 teaspoon soda	2 eggs
1 teaspoon salt	1 cup cooked pumpkin
½ teaspoon cinnamon	⅓ cup water
½ teaspoon nutmeg	½ cup chopped pecans
⅓ cup shortening	

Preheat oven to 350°. Grease a 9½ x 5¼-inch loaf pan. Sift together flour, baking powder, soda, salt, cinnamon, and nutmeg. Set aside. Cream shortening, sugar, and vanilla extract. Add eggs, one at a time, beating thoroughly after each addition. Stir in pumpkin. Stir in dry ingredients in 4 additions, alternating with water until just smooth. Add chopped nuts and pour into loaf pan. Bake for 40-45 minutes. Turn out on rack and cool right side up. Serve at room temperature.

This is good with softened cream cheese.

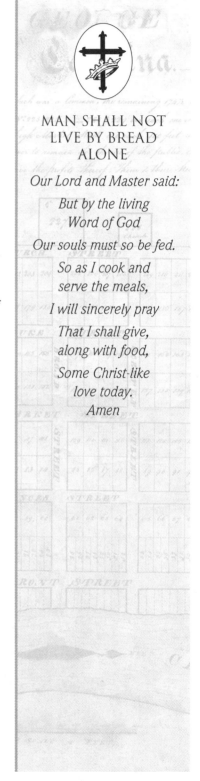

MAN SHALL NOT
LIVE BY BREAD
ALONE

Our Lord and Master said:

*But by the living
Word of God*

Our souls must so be fed.

*So as I cook and
serve the meals,*

I will sincerely pray

*That I shall give,
along with food,*

*Some Christ-like
love today.*

Amen

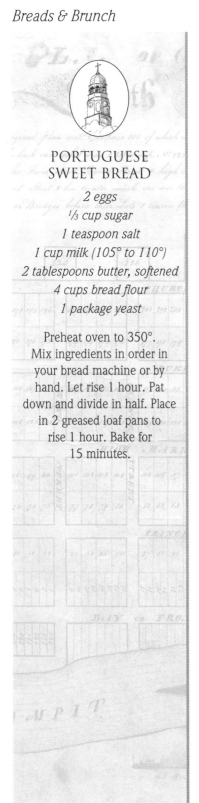

PORTUGUESE SWEET BREAD

2 eggs

⅓ cup sugar

1 teaspoon salt

1 cup milk (105° to 110°)

2 tablespoons butter, softened

4 cups bread flour

1 package yeast

Preheat oven to 350°. Mix ingredients in order in your bread machine or by hand. Let rise 1 hour. Pat down and divide in half. Place in 2 greased loaf pans to rise 1 hour. Bake for 15 minutes.

CRANBERRY NUT BREAD

2	cups all-purpose sifted flour	¾	cup orange juice
1	cup sugar	1	tablespoon grated orange rind
1½	teaspoons baking powder	1	egg, well beaten
½	teaspoon baking soda	½	cup chopped nuts
1	teaspoon salt	2	cups cranberries, coarsely chopped
¼	cup shortening		

Preheat oven to 350°. Sift together dry ingredients. Cut in shortening with a pastry blender or 2 knives until mixture resembles coarse cornmeal. Make a well in the center. Combine orange juice and grated rind with well-beaten egg. Pour all at once into dry ingredients, mix just enough to dampen. Carefully fold in nuts and cranberries. Spoon into greased loaf pan. Spread corners and sides slightly higher than center. Bake for about 1 hour or until crust is golden brown and toothpick inserted comes out clean. Remove from pan. Cool. Store overnight for easy slicing.

If using frozen cranberries, do not thaw. Quick rinse and chop while frozen.

For easy removal, line loaf pan with parchment paper letting paper hang over sides by 2 inches.

HERB BREAD

1	package dry yeast	2	teaspoons dill
¼	cup warm water	1	tablespoon melted butter
1	cup small curd cottage cheese	¼	teaspoon baking soda
2	tablespoons sugar	1	teaspoon salt
2	teaspoons chopped green onion	1	egg
		2¼	cups flour

Preheat oven to 350°. Dissolve yeast in water and set aside. Heat cottage cheese to lukewarm. Combine in a large bowl with sugar, onion, dill, butter, soda, salt, egg, and yeast. Add flour to form a soft dough, beating well. Cover; let rise until doubled. Beat down and place in a greased 8½x4½-inch bread pan; let rise again until doubled. Bake for 40 minutes.

Monterey Bread

1 loaf of French bread	1 cup grated Parmesan cheese
1 cup mayonnaise	3 tablespoons grated onion

Preheat oven to 350°. Slice bread in half lengthwise. Lay each half on foil and crimp around it. Mix mayonnaise, cheese, and onion; spread on halves of bread. Bake until top is brown and bubbly, slice and serve.

Hellmann's mayonnaise was recommended for this recipe.

Irish Soda Bread

2 cups all-purpose flour	¼ cup raisins
1 teaspoon baking powder	1 egg white, slightly beaten
½ teaspoon baking soda	¾ cup buttermilk
1/16 teaspoon salt	Vegetable cooking spray
3 tablespoons butter	

Preheat oven to 375°. Mix together flour, baking powder, baking soda, and salt. Cut in butter until mixture is course and crumbly. Add raisins. Make a well in center of mixture. In small bowl, mix egg white and buttermilk. Combine with dry mixture. Knead dough on a lightly floured surface for 1 minute. Shape into 7-inch round loaf. Spray vegetable cooking spray on baking sheet. Place dough on sheet. Cut an "X" on the top with a sharp knife about ¼-inch deep. Bake 30 minutes.

Yield: 4 servings.

BUTTERMILK

Buttermilk is not loaded with fat. It is called that, because it refers to the milky liquid that is left after butter has been churned from milk. It is a thick nutritious drink that is lower in fat than whole milk or cream, and is higher in potassium, calcium, and vitamin B-12. Like yogurt and sour cream, it is an acidic ingredient that gives baked goods body and soft texture.

Use buttermilk as a substitute to help trim down the calories in prepared dishes. Use it instead of an egg when breading chicken or fish. When mashing potatoes, use it instead of butter and milk.

FOR *the Lord your God is bringing you into a good land. A land of wheat and barley, of vines and fig trees and pomegranates, a land of olive oil and honey; a land where you shall eat food without scarcity, in which you shall not lack anything. Deuteronomy 8:7-9*

CAPPUCCINO MUFFINS

3	cups all-purpose flour		6	tablespoons melted butter
1	cup sugar		2	large eggs, at room temperature
1	tablespoon baking powder			
½	teaspoon baking soda		4	teaspoons instant espresso powder
½	teaspoon salt			
¼	teaspoon cinnamon		1⅔	cups buttermilk, at room temperature

Preheat oven to 375°. Lightly coat twelve 2 ½-inch deep, or 24 smaller-size muffin pan cups with cooking spray. Set aside. In medium bowl, whisk together flour, sugar, baking powder, baking soda, salt, and cinnamon. In a large bowl, whisk butter, eggs, and espresso powder until smooth. Stir in half of flour mixture until just moistened. Stir in half of buttermilk and half of remaining flour mixture; then stir in remaining buttermilk and flour mixture. Divide batter among prepared cups.

TOPPING

¼	cup all-purpose flour		¼	teaspoon cinnamon
2	tablespoons sugar		2	tablespoons butter

Combine flour, sugar, and cinnamon; cut in butter and squeeze mixture to form clumps. Sprinkle mixture on muffins. Bake muffins until a toothpick inserted in center comes out clean, 15-25 minutes. Cool in pan on wire rack 5 minutes, then transfer muffins to rack to cool.

Yield: 12 large or 24 smaller muffins.

WHOLE WHEAT APRICOT MUFFINS

1	cup all-purpose flour	1	cup buttermilk
⅔	cup whole wheat flour	¼	cup melted butter
½	cup sugar	½	teaspoon vanilla extract
1¼	teaspoons grated orange rind	1	large egg
1	teaspoon baking soda	1	cup finely chopped dried apricots
¼	teaspoon salt		Vegetable cooking spray

Preheat oven to 375°. Lightly spoon flours into dry measuring cups, level with a knife. Combine flours, sugar, orange rind, baking soda, and salt in a large bowl, stirring with a whisk; make a well in center of mixture. Combine buttermilk, butter, vanilla extract, and egg; add to flour mixture, stirring just until moist. Fold in apricots. Spoon batter into 12 muffin cups coated with cooking spray. Bake for 15 minutes or until muffins spring back when touched lightly in center. Remove muffins from pan and place on a wire rack.

Yield: 1 dozen.

ASHLEY'S BUNS

½	cup melted butter	1	cup raisins
2	cups self-rising flour		2% milk
½	cup sugar	1¼	cups powdered sugar
1	tablespoon cinnamon	1	tablespoon vanilla extract

Preheat oven to 450°. Melt butter and pour into a 7x11-inch loaf pan. Hand mix flour, sugar, cinnamon, and raisins. Slowly add enough milk until a sticky dough is achieved. Scoop dough with soup spoon and push dough down into the loaf pan. Bake 15 minutes. Mix powdered sugar, vanilla extract, and enough milk to make a glaze the consistency of honey. Glaze buns when cool.

Yield: 8-10 servings.

WHOLE WHEAT BREAD

2 cups white flour
2 cups whole wheat flour
$\frac{1}{16}$ teaspoon salt
1 teaspoon baking soda
Buttermilk

Preheat oven to 300°.
Mix flour, salt, and baking soda together. Add enough buttermilk to form dough. Form into round loaf; bake for 45 minutes.

Hilda G. Daunt

BEST RAISIN BRAN MUFFINS

2½ cups all purpose flour
1 teaspoon salt
2½ teaspoons baking soda
1 teaspoon ground cinnamon
1¼ cups + 2 tablespoons sugar
7½ ounces (½ of 15 ounce package) lightly crushed raisin bran cereal
2 (8 ounce) cartons plain low-fat yogurt

2 eggs, beaten
½ cup vegetable oil
1½ tablespoons orange rind, grated OR 1½ tablespoons dried orange peel
½ cup chopped nuts (pecans or walnuts or combination)
Ground cinnamon for sprinkling

Preheat oven to 375°. In a large bowl, combine first 5 ingredients. Add the crushed raisin bran cereal. In a separate bowl, mix the yogurt, beaten eggs, and oil. Combine well with flour mixture. Add the orange peel and nuts. Stir mixture. Put dough in greased muffin tins (⅔ full), sprinkle with cinnamon and bake for approximately 20 minutes for standard size cups (add a few minutes for cold dough). Paper liners can be used in lieu of greasing tins.

Yield: 18 plus as desired.

Refrigerate dough in a container with a tight lid (keeps well within the use date of the yogurt). Whenever you want fresh muffins, bake as many as desired.

SPOON ROLLS

1 tablespoon dry yeast
2 cups warm water
1 egg, beaten

½-¾ cup sugar
¾ cup light oil
4 cups self-rising flour

Preheat oven to 400°. Dissolve yeast in warm water. Add egg, sugar, and oil to yeast mixture. Mix well. Then add the flour (mixture will be soupy). Grease 24 muffin tins with oil or nonstick spray. Fill muffin tin to ⅔ full. Bake for 8-10 minutes.

Yield: 2 dozen.

Absolutely delicious and easy to make — a yeast muffin!

ORANGE ROLLS

1 package dry yeast
½ cup warm water
   (100° to 110°)
1 cup sugar, divided
½ cup sour cream
2 tablespoons butter, softened
½ teaspoon salt

1 large egg, lightly beaten
3½ cups all-purpose flour,
   divided
Vegetable cooking spray
2 tablespoons melted butter
3 tablespoons grated orange
   rind

Preheat oven to 350°. To prepare dough, dissolve yeast in warm water in a large bowl; let stand 5 minutes. Add ¼ cup sugar, sour cream, butter, salt, and egg. Beat with a mixer at medium speed until smooth. Lightly spoon flour into dry measuring cups, level with a knife. Add 2 cups flour to yeast mixture; beat until smooth. Add 1 cup to flour yeast mixture, stirring until a soft dough forms. Turn dough out onto a floured surface. Knead until smooth and elastic (about 10 minutes), add enough remaining flour, 1 tablespoon at a time, to prevent dough from sticking to hand (dough will feel sticky). Place dough in a large bowl coated with cooking spray, turning to coat top. Cover and let rise in a warm place (85°), free from drafts, 1 hour and 15 minutes or until doubled in size. Gently press two fingers into dough. If indentation remains, dough has risen enough. Punch dough down, cover and let rest 5 minutes. Divide dough in half. Working with 1 portion at a time (cover remaining dough to prevent drying), roll each portion of dough into a 12-inch circle on a floured surface. Brush surface of each circle with 1 tablespoon melted butter. Combine ¾ cup sugar and rind. Sprinkle half of sugar mixture over each circle. Cut each circle into 12 wedges. Roll up each wedge tightly, beginning at wide end. Place rolls, point sides down, in a 13x9-inch baking pan coated with cooking spray. Cover and let rise 25 minutes or until doubled in size. Uncover dough and bake for 25 minutes or until golden brown.

GLAZE

¾ cup sugar
¼ cup butter

2 tablespoons fresh orange
   juice
½ cup sour cream

While rolls bake, combine sugar, butter, and orange juice in a small saucepan; bring to a boil over medium-high heat. Cook 3 minutes or until sugar dissolves, stirring occasionally. Remove from heat, cool slightly. Stir in sour cream. Drizzle glaze over warm rolls, let stand 20 minutes before serving.

Yield: 2 dozen.

ROLLS

1 yeast cake
½ cup warm water
1 tablespoon salt
⅔ cup sugar
*5 heaping tablespoons solid
shortening*
2 eggs
¾ cup warm water
6 cups unsifted flour

Preheat oven to 350°. Dissolve yeast in ½ cup warm water. Add salt, sugar, shortening, eggs, beating in each. Add ¾ cup warm water. Beat 2 minutes. Sift and add half of flour. Beat 3 minutes. Add other half of sifted flour. Mix well, cover, let rise once, push down, and keep in refrigerator until ready to use. Shape in balls about the size of a walnut, cover lightly with vegetable oil. Allow dough to rise about 2 or 3 hours. Bake for 25 minutes or until golden brown.

Yield: 3-4 dozen.

Leila Ford

LEMON CURD

2 lemons
½ cup unsalted butter
1 cup sugar
2 eggs, beaten

Grate and squeeze lemons;
reserve peel and juice. In
a small saucepan, melt
butter. Add sugar; cook until
dissolved. With wire whisk,
beat in eggs, lemon juice, and
peel; cook until mixture is
thick and coats back of spoon.
Cover; refrigerate.

SCONES

2	cups flour	3	tablespoons unsalted butter, cut into pieces
2	tablespoons sugar		
2	tablespoons baking powder	1	cup heavy cream

Preheat oven to 375°. In a large bowl, combine flour, sugar, and baking powder; mix well. Using pastry blender, cut in butter until crumbly. Add cream; mix until dough forms. On a floured surface, knead dough 5-6 times. Form into an 8-inch circle; place on ungreased cookie sheet. Cut into 8 wedges; do not separate. Bake for 18-23 minutes or until light golden brown. Cut into wedges; serve warm with butter and lemon curd, if desired.

APRICOT, WHITE CHOCOLATE, AND WALNUT SCONES

2	cups flour	6	(1 ounce) squares of white chocolate, cut into ½-inch chunks
⅓	cup sugar		
2	teaspoons baking powder		
½	teaspoon salt	1	cup coarsely broken, toasted walnuts (see note)
¼	cup salted butter, chilled		
½	cup whipping cream		
1	large egg	1	cup finely chopped dried apricots
1½	teaspoons vanilla extract		

Preheat oven to 375°. In a large bowl, stir together the flour, sugar, baking powder, and salt. Cut the butter into ½-inch cubes and distribute them over the flour mixture. With a pastry blender or two knives used scissors fashion, cut in the butter until the mixture resembles coarse crumbs. In a small bowl, stir together the cream, egg, and vanilla extract. Add the cream mixture to the flour mixture and knead until combined. Knead in the white chocolate, walnuts and apricots. With lightly floured hands, pat the dough out into a 9-inch diameter circle in the center of an ungreased baking sheet. With a serrated knife, cut circle into 8 wedges. Bake for 15-20 minutes, or until the top is lightly browned. Remove the baking sheet to a wire rack and cool for 5 minutes. Using a spatula, transfer the scones to the wire rack to cool. Cut wedges again, if necessary. Serve warm or cool completely. Store in an airtight container.

To toast walnuts, place the walnuts in a single layer on a baking sheet and bake at 375° for 5-7 minutes, shaking the sheet a couple times, until the nuts are fragrant.

CRANBERRY SCONES

2	cups all-purpose flour	½	teaspoon baking soda
¾	cup dried cranberries	½	teaspoon salt
⅓	cup cornmeal	½	teaspoon ground nutmeg
¼	cup plus 1 tablespoon sugar, divided	2	egg whites, lightly beaten
2	teaspoons baking powder	⅔	cup buttermilk
1	tablespoon grated orange peel	¼	cup oil
			Vegetable cooking spray

Preheat oven to 400°. In a large bowl, combine the flour, cranberries, cornmeal, ¼ cup sugar, baking powder, orange peel, baking soda, salt, and nutmeg. In another bowl, combine the egg whites, buttermilk, and oil. Add to dry ingredients and stir until a soft dough forms. On a floured surface, gently knead 6-8 times. Pat dough into an 8 ½-inch circle. Place on a baking sheet coated with nonstick cooking spray. Cut into 12 wedges; do not separate. Sprinkle with remaining sugar. Bake for 15-17 minutes or until golden brown. Remove to wire rack. Serve warm.

Yield: 1 dozen.

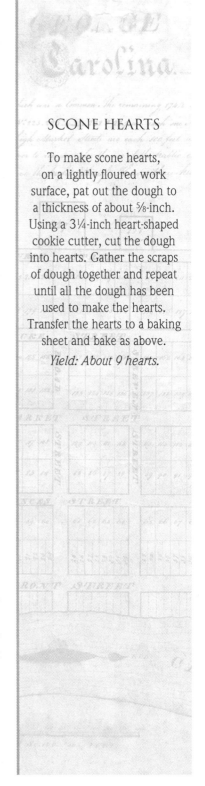

SCONE HEARTS

To make scone hearts, on a lightly floured work surface, pat out the dough to a thickness of about ⅝-inch. Using a 3¼-inch heart-shaped cookie cutter, cut the dough into hearts. Gather the scraps of dough together and repeat until all the dough has been used to make the hearts. Transfer the hearts to a baking sheet and bake as above.

Yield: About 9 hearts.

RED LOBSTER CHEESE GARLIC BISCUITS

2	cups buttermilk baking mix	½	cup shredded Cheddar cheese
⅔	cup milk	¼	cup butter, melted
		¼	teaspoon garlic powder

Preheat oven to 450°. Combine buttermilk baking mix, milk, and cheese with a wooden spoon until soft dough forms. Beat vigorously 30 seconds. Drop dough by heaping tablespoon onto an ungreased cookie sheet. Bake 8-10 minutes or until golden brown. Combine melted butter and garlic powder. Brush over warm biscuit before removing from cookie sheet. Serve warm.

Yield: 10-12 biscuits.

Bisquick was recommended for this recipe.

CORNMEAL

Cornmeal has a sweet yet robust flavor, making it a great ingredient for many dishes.

On its own, it is relatively low in fat (about 2-3 grams per 100 grams of cornmeal). And, since most cornmeal has been enriched with iron and B vitamins, it's also a great source of energy.

Although it is widely available in steel-ground varieties at the grocery store, connoisseurs recommend the stone-ground cornmeal that is available in many natural food stores. Slightly more perishable, it's said to have extra flavor and nutrition.

Store cornmeal in a cool dry place in an airtight container. Most cornmeal will keep this way for up to 1 year.

SWEET POTATO BISCUITS

2	cups self-rising flour	3	tablespoons shortening
¼	cup packed brown sugar	1	cup mashed sweet
1	teaspoon ground cinnamon		potatoes
1	teaspoon ground ginger	6	tablespoons milk
8	tablespoons cold butter, divided		

Preheat oven to 425°. In a bowl, combine the flour, brown sugar, cinnamon, and ginger. Cut in 4 tablespoons butter and shortening until mixture resembles coarse crumbs. In another bowl, combine sweet potatoes and milk; stir into crumb mixture just until combined. Turn onto a floured surface; knead 8-10 times. Roll to ½-inch thickness; cut with a 2½-inch biscuit cutter. Place on ungreased baking sheet. Melt remaining butter; brush over dough. Bake for 10-12 minutes or until golden brown. Remove to wire racks. Serve warm.

Yield: 1½ dozen.

As a substitute for each cup of self-rising flour, place 1½ teaspoons baking powder and ½ teaspoon salt in a measuring cup. Add all-purpose flour to measure 1 cup.

ALMOST HOMEMADE BISCUITS

2	cups biscuit baking mix	1	cup whipping cream

Preheat oven to 425°. Stir whipping cream into biscuit baking mix. Drop by large tablespoon onto greased cookie sheet, or roll in a light coating of flour and cut into 2-inch rounds. Bake approximately 12 minutes.

Bisquick biscuit baking mix was recommended for this recipe.

CHEESE BISCUITS

½	cup butter	1	cup grated Cheddar cheese
2	cups biscuit baking mix	1	cup sour cream

Cut butter into biscuit baking mix with a pastry cutter. Stir in cheese and sour cream. Drop by large tablespoon onto greased cookie sheet, or roll in a light coating of flour and cut into 2-inch rounds. Bake approximately 12 minutes.

BISCUITS

2	cups all-purpose flour	1/2	cup frozen butter, grated
1	teaspoon salt	1	cup milk or buttermilk
2	teaspoons baking powder		

Preheat oven to 450°. Hand mix flour, salt, and baking powder. Hand grate in butter, mixing periodically. Add a portion of milk and mix; repeat until a dough is achieved. Place dough on floured surface, and hand flatten and fold 4 or 5 times. Roll to ½-inch thick, cut with cookie cutter to desired shape. Bake for 15 minutes on lightly greased cookie sheet.

CORNBREAD

1	(15 ounce) can creamed corn	1	(8 ounce) carton sour cream
2	(8½ ounce) boxes cornbread mix	½	cup vegetable oil
		3	eggs
		½	cup sugar

Preheat oven to 375°. Mix ingredients together. Pour in a greased 9x13-inch pan. Bake for 35-45 minutes.

Yield: 12 servings.

CHEESE-ONION CORN BREAD

1½	cups chopped onions	½	cup milk
¼	cup butter, melted	1	(8½ ounce) package corn muffin mix
1	cup sour cream	1	(8 ounce) can cream style corn
¼	teaspoon salt	2	drops red pepper sauce, optional
1	cup sharp Cheddar cheese, shredded and divided		
1	egg, beaten		

Preheat oven to 425°. Sauté onions in butter for 10 minutes. Cool slightly. Add the sour cream, salt, and ½ cup cheese to onion mixture and set aside. In a separate bowl, mix together the egg, milk, muffin mix, corn, and red pepper sauce. Spread muffin mix in an 8-inch square greased pan. Put the sour cream mixture on top. Sprinkle the rest of the cheese on top. Bake for 30-35 minutes. Let set before cutting.

SOUTHERN CORN BREAD

2 cups white cornmeal
2½ cups boiling water
1½ tablespoons butter, melted
1½ teaspoons salt
2 egg yolks, slightly beaten
1½ cups buttermilk
1 teaspoon baking soda
2 egg whites, beaten until stiff

Preheat oven to 400°. Add cornmeal gradually to boiling water and let stand until cool. Add butter, salt, slightly beaten egg yolks, and buttermilk mixed with baking soda. Beat 2 minutes and add whites of eggs. Turn into a greased baking dish and bake for 40 minutes.

Irene Davis

EASY MEXICAN CORNBREAD

	Canola oil	1	(11 ounce) can corn and pepper mix, not drained
2	eggs	1	(8 ounce) package processed cheese loaf, shredded
⅔	cup milk		
2	(8½ ounce) boxes corn muffin mix		
1	(4½ ounce) can chopped green chilies, not drained		

Preheat oven to 400°. Place enough oil in the bottom of 9x13-inch pan to cover and put it in the oven to get hot as the oven heats. Mix the eggs and milk and pour over the corn muffin mix in a large bowl. Add all the other ingredients and stir. You may need to add a little more milk if the batter seems too thick. Let the batter rest while the oven and pan heat up! Pour the batter into the hot pan and bake until the top is golden brown, approximately 20-25 minutes.

Yield: 12 servings.

BAKED APPLE FRENCH TOAST

½	cup butter	12	slices firm bread
3	large green apples	8	eggs
½	cup brown sugar	4	cups milk
1	tablespoon water	2	tablespoons vanilla extract
12	ounces cream cheese		Cinnamon

Preheat oven to 350°. Set rack in lower third of oven. Butter a 9x13-inch baking pan. Core and cut apples into thin wedges, leaving skin on. In a skillet, melt butter with brown sugar and 1 tablespoon of water. Add apples and cook, stirring for 2 to 3 minutes. Transfer to the baking dish and let cool. Cut cream cheese into cubes and arrange evenly over the apples. Cut the slices of bread in half diagonally and layer over the apples to cover the whole dish. Bread will overlap.

In a large mixing bowl, beat together eggs, milk, and vanilla extract. Pour the egg mixture over the bread, taking care to dampen all the bread. Sprinkle with cinnamon. Bake 40-50 minutes until golden and puffed. Let cool 10 minutes before serving. This reheats beautifully.

Yield: 8-12 servings.

Use white, wheat, French, sourdough, cinnamon, or raisin bread.

RUFFLED HAM AND EGGS

¾   pound finely chopped
     mushrooms
¼   cup finely chopped shallots
2   tablespoons unsalted
     butter
½   teaspoon salt
¼   teaspoon black pepper
2   tablespoons crème fraîche
     or sour cream

1   tablespoon finely chopped
     fresh tarragon
12   slices Black Forest ham
     or Virginia ham, thinly
     sliced
12   large eggs
     Half-and-half

Preheat oven to 400°. Cook mushrooms and shallots in butter with salt and pepper in a large heavy skillet over moderately high heat. Stir until mushrooms are tender and the liquid they give off has evaporated, about 10 minutes. Remove from heat and stir in crème fraîche/sour cream and tarragon. Fit 1 slice of ham into each of 12 slightly oiled (½ cup) muffin cups. Ends will stick up and hang over edges of cups. Divide mushroom mixture among cups and crack 1 egg into each. Pour 1 teaspoon half-and-half over top. Bake in middle of oven until whites are cooked but yolks are still runny, about 15 minutes. Season eggs with salt and pepper and remove with ham from muffin cups carefully, using 2 spoons or small spatulas. Garnish with fresh tarragon. Serve with buttered brioche or challah toast.

Yield: 12 servings.

BAKED GRITS AND SAUSAGE

3   cups cooked, cooled grits
1   teaspoon salt
1   pound bulk sausage
1½   cups hot milk

3   eggs, beaten
3   tablespoons butter
1¼   cups grated extra sharp
     Cheddar cheese

Preheat oven to 350°. Prepare grits with salt according to package cooking directions. Brown sausage and drain well on brown paper. Place sausage in large greased ovenproof casserole dish. Mix grits, milk, eggs, butter, and cheese together. Pour over sausage. Bake 1 hour.

Yield: 8-10 servings

Can be made the day before and refrigerated.

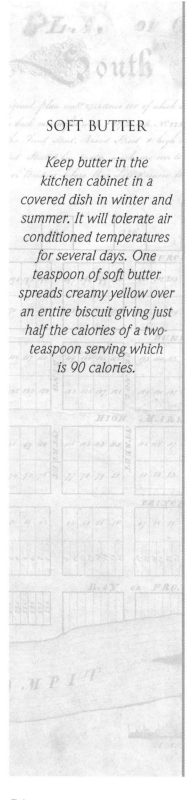

SOFT BUTTER

Keep butter in the kitchen cabinet in a covered dish in winter and summer. It will tolerate air conditioned temperatures for several days. One teaspoon of soft butter spreads creamy yellow over an entire biscuit giving just half the calories of a two-teaspoon serving which is 90 calories.

BROCCOLI AND CHEESE PIE

CRUST

⅓	cup yellow cornmeal		⅓	cup milk
⅓	cup all-purpose flour		1	large egg
1½	teaspoons baking powder			

Preheat oven to 350°. Grease a deep 9-inch pie pan. In a medium-size bowl, combine the cornmeal, flour, and baking powder. In a small bowl, whisk together the milk and egg. Add the milk mixture to the dry ingredients, stirring until just blended. Using the back of a spoon, spread the dough evenly over the bottom and sides of the prepared pan. Bake for 10 minutes, or until crust is set. Remove the pan from the oven and set aside.

FILLING

1	(6 ounce) package raw broccoli florets		⅓	cup large curd cottage cheese
1	tablespoon salted butter		⅛	teaspoon salt, or to taste
½	cup finely chopped yellow onion		⅛	teaspoon coarsely ground black pepper
3	large eggs		⅛	teaspoon ground nutmeg
1	cup shredded sharp Cheddar cheese			

Bring a medium-size saucepan of water to a boil over high heat. Cook broccoli in boiling water for 2 minutes or until crisp-tender. Drain well, rinse under cold running water and drain again. Reserve a few florets for garnish. Coarsely chop remaining broccoli and place in a large bowl. In a small saucepan over moderate heat, melt the butter. Add the onion and sauté for 5 minutes or until onion is translucent. Add the onion, eggs, Cheddar cheese, cottage cheese, salt, and pepper to the bowl with the broccoli. Stir until well blended. Spoon filling into the prepared crust. Sprinkle with nutmeg. Bake for 35-40 minutes or until a utility knife inserted in the center comes out clean. Remove the pie from the oven and place on a wire rack to cool for 5 minutes. Garnish with reserved florets if desired. Cut into wedges. Serve pie immediately.

Yield: 6 servings.

Variation: Making a pie crust pastry

1⅓	cups flour		½	cup cold solid vegetable shortening
½	teaspoon salt		3	tablespoons cold water

Combine flour and salt. Cut in shortening. Add water 1 tablespoon at a time; toss with fork. Work dough into a ball. Roll out on lightly floured board. Place in 9-inch pie pan.

EGG MUFFINS

1 dozen eggs, hard boiled
    and diced
1 pound sharp Cheddar
    cheese, grated
1 medium onion, diced
½ pound bacon, fried,
    drained, and crumbled
    Worcestershire sauce, to
    taste

1 tablespoon spicy mustard
    Few drops hot pepper
    sauce
¼ teaspoon freshly ground
    black pepper
¼ teaspoon garlic powder
    Mayonnaise
    Parmesan cheese
8 English muffins, split

Mix eggs, cheese, onion, and bacon. Add Worcestershire sauce, mustard, hot pepper sauce, pepper, and garlic powder. Add mayonnaise to make consistency of chicken salad. Mix well. *At time of serving, preheat broiler. Spoon mixture onto English muffin halves and sprinkle with Parmesan cheese. Broil under broiler until hot and bubbly.

Yield: 16 servings.

*This may be prepared ahead up to this point and stored, covered in refrigerator up to 2 weeks.

Add some fruit, orange juice, maybe a sweet roll and lots of coffee, and the party continues!!

This can be halved for week-end guests' breakfast.

OPEN FACE CRAB MUFFINS

1 pound fresh lump
    crabmeat
    White pepper to taste
⅓ cup ranch dressing
1 teaspoon lemon juice
6 green onions, finely
    chopped, white only

6 English muffins, split
    Mayonnaise, optional
    Green leaf lettuce,
    chopped
8 thick sliced tomatoes
8 slices baby Swiss cheese
    Vegetable cooking spray

Preheat oven to 350°. Season crabmeat with pepper, ranch dressing, lemon juice, and green onions. Toss and set aside. Lightly toast English muffins. Lightly spread each slice of muffins with dressing and mayonnaise. Top each muffin with crabmeat mixture. Add lettuce and tomatoes to each and top with slice of cheese. Place on baking sheet which has been sprayed with vegetable cooking spray. Bake for 20 minutes or until cheese melts.

Yield: 12 servings.

HOMEMADE CRÈME FRAÎCHE: 2 VARIATIONS

First Variation
1 cup whipping cream
2 tablespoons buttermilk

Combine whipping cream with buttermilk. Cover and let stand at room temperature overnight or until thick.

Second Variation
½ cup heavy whipping cream
½ cup sour cream

Whisk together whipping cream and sour cream. Pour the mixture into a jar, cover and let stand in a warm place for 12 hours. Then stir and refrigerate for 24 hours.

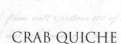

CRAB QUICHE

*1 cup shredded natural
Swiss cheese*

1 (9-inch) unbaked pie shell

8 ounces crabmeat

*2 green onions with tops,
sliced*

3 eggs, beaten

1 cup cream

½ teaspoon salt

*½ teaspoon grated lemon
peel, or lemon juice*

¼ teaspoon dry mustard

¼ cup slivered almonds

Preheat oven to 325°.
Arrange cheese evenly over
bottom of 9 inch pie shell.
Distribute crabmeat over
shell and sprinkle with green
onions. Combine beaten eggs,
cream, salt, lemon, and dry
mustard. Pour evenly over
crabmeat. Top with slivered
almonds. Bake for 45-60
minutes or until set. Let stand
10 minutes before serving.

Yield: 6-8 servings.

**Diced or shredded
imitation crabmeat may
be used as a substitute
for fresh crabmeat.**

CREAMY GRITS

LOUIS'S AT PAWLEYS, PAWLEYS ISLAND, SC

2	cups whole milk	4	tablespoons unsalted butter
2	cups water	1	cup heavy cream
1	teaspoon salt	2	teaspoons freshly ground black pepper
1	cup uncooked quick cooking grits, not instant		

Bring the milk and water to a boil in a heavy-bottomed saucepan over medium heat. Stir in the salt. Slowly add the grits, stirring constantly. When the grits begin to thicken, turn the heat down to low and simmer for 30-40 minutes, stirring occasionally to prevent the grits from scorching. Add the butter and cream, stirring to incorporate thoroughly and simmer for 5 minutes. Stir in the pepper. Serve the grits immediately or keep them warm, covered, in a double boiler over simmering water.

Yield: 6 cups.

If the grits are too thick, stir in more cream or milk. Remember that grits solidify as the cool; they will get thicker once on the plates.

BLT BREAKFAST SANDWICH

1	(0.9-ounce) envelope hollandaise sauce mix	¾	teaspoon seasoned pepper, divided
6	bacon slices, cooked and crumbled	4	bread slices, toasted
2	(3 ounce) packages cream cheese, softened	1	tablespoon butter
		4	large eggs
2	tablespoons chopped fresh chives	4	lettuce leaves
		2	small tomatoes, sliced

Prepare hollandaise sauce according to package directions; keep warm. Stir together bacon, cream cheese, chives, and ¼ teaspoon seasoned pepper; spread evenly on one side of each toasted bread slice. Melt butter in a large non-stick skillet over medium heat. Gently break eggs into hot skillet and sprinkle evenly with ¼ teaspoon seasoned pepper. Cook 2-3 minutes on each side or until done. Place lettuce leaves and tomatoes on top of bread slices and top with fried eggs. Drizzle hollandaise sauce evenly over top and sprinkle evenly with remaining ¼ teaspoon seasoned pepper. Serve immediately.

Yield: 4 servings.

BREAKFAST PIZZA

2	cups frozen shredded hash brown potatoes	2	tablespoons diced sweet red pepper
¼	teaspoon ground cumin	1	tablespoon finely chopped jalapeño pepper, optional
¼	teaspoon chili powder	1	garlic clove, minced
2	tablespoons oil, divided	1	prebaked pizza shell crust
6	eggs	½	cup salsa
2	tablespoons milk	¾	cup shredded Cheddar cheese
¼	teaspoon salt		
2	green onions, chopped, white part only		

Preheat oven to 375°. In a nonstick skillet, cook hash browns, cumin, and chili powder in 1 tablespoon oil over medium heat until golden. Remove and keep warm. In a bowl, beat eggs, milk, and salt. Set aside. In the same skillet, sauté the onions, peppers, and garlic in remaining oil until tender. Add egg mixture. Cook and stir over medium heat until almost set. Remove from the heat. Place crust on an ungreased 14-inch pizza pan. Spread salsa over crust. Top with egg mixture. Sprinkle with hash browns and cheese. Bake 8-10 minutes or until cheese is melted.

Yield: 6 slices.

Pizza crust can also be found in the dairy section in tubes. Follow stretching directions but bake for ¹/₂ of the time.

BAKED CHICKEN SANDWICHES

1	pound fresh mushrooms, sliced	⅓	cup ripe chopped olives
¼	cup butter, softened	¾	cup mayonnaise
16	slices white bread, crust removed	2	tablespoons chopped onion
2	cups cooked, cut up white chicken meat	1	(10½ ounce) can cream of chicken soup
3	eggs, hard-boiled and chopped	1	cup sour cream
		2	tablespoons sherry
			Paprika to sprinkle on top

Preheat oven to 325°. Sauté mushrooms in 2 tablespoons butter. Butter both sides of bread with remaining butter and place 8 slices in 9x13-inch baking dish. Cover bread with a mixture of mushrooms, chicken, eggs, olives, mayonnaise, and onion. Arrange other slices of bread on top. Combine soup, sour cream, and sherry. Pour on top. Bake for 30-45 minutes.

Yield: 8 servings.

REUBEN MUFFINS

4 English muffins, split and toasted

1 pound corned beef, cooked and sliced

2 cups sauerkraut, well drained

½ cup Russian dressing

8 slices Swiss cheese, halved

Top each muffin half with corned beef, sauerkraut, dressing, and cheese. Broil 6 inches from heat 2 minutes or until cheese melts.

Yield: 4 servings.

GERMAN PANCAKES

4	tablespoons butter	1	teaspoon vanilla extract
6	eggs	2	teaspoons baking powder
1	cup flour	1	teaspoon salt
1	cup milk		

Preheat oven to 450°. Put 2 tablespoons butter in each of two pie tins. Melt in oven. Beat eggs, flour, milk, vanilla extract, baking powder, and salt. Beat until smooth. Pour ½ into each pie tin. Bake for 25 minutes or until edges are brown. Serve warm.

Yield: 4-6 servings.

COTTAGE CHEESE PANCAKES

3	large eggs, separated	2	tablespoons oil
¼	cup all-purpose flour	1	cup small curd cottage cheese
¼	teaspoon salt		

Beat egg whites and set aside. Beat yolks and add other ingredients. Fold in the beaten egg whites. Cook pancakes as usual.

Yield: 2 servings.

SWEDISH PANCAKES

4	eggs, beaten	2	cups plain flour, sifted
2	cups milk	½	cup butter, melted
½	cup sugar		Jelly to top
1/16	teaspoon salt		

Mix eggs, milk, sugar, salt, and flour. Add butter last. Lightly grease frying pan. Pour in ⅓ cup batter (cooks like a crêpe). Flip when it begins to brown. Roll up on warming plate. Spread 1 teaspoon jelly down center. Roll back up.

Yield: 5 servings.

WAFFLES

2	cups flour	2	eggs	
4	teaspoons baking powder	1½	cups milk	
¾	teaspoon salt	1	tablespoon corn oil	

Sift together flour, baking powder, and salt. Separate eggs. Add milk to egg yolks and add to dry mixture. Beat egg whites until stiff and fold in to mixture. Corn oil may be added. Cook according to directions on your waffle grill.

CHEESE GRITS

4	cups boiling water	¼	cup butter
1	teaspoon salt	2	cups or more grated sharp cheese
1	cup quick cooking grits, not instant	3	eggs, well beaten

Preheat oven to 350°. Slowly pour the grits into the boiling, salted water, stirring constantly until mixed. Cook 2½-5 minutes, stirring occasionally. When grits are cooked, add butter, cheese, and eggs. Mix well. Pour into greased 1½-quart baking dish and bake 30-40 minutes.

Yield: 8-10 servings.

HE makes grass grow for the cattle, and the plants for men to cultivate bringing forth food from the earth: wine that gladdens the heart of man, oil to make his face shine, and bread that sustains his heart. *Psalm 104:14,15*

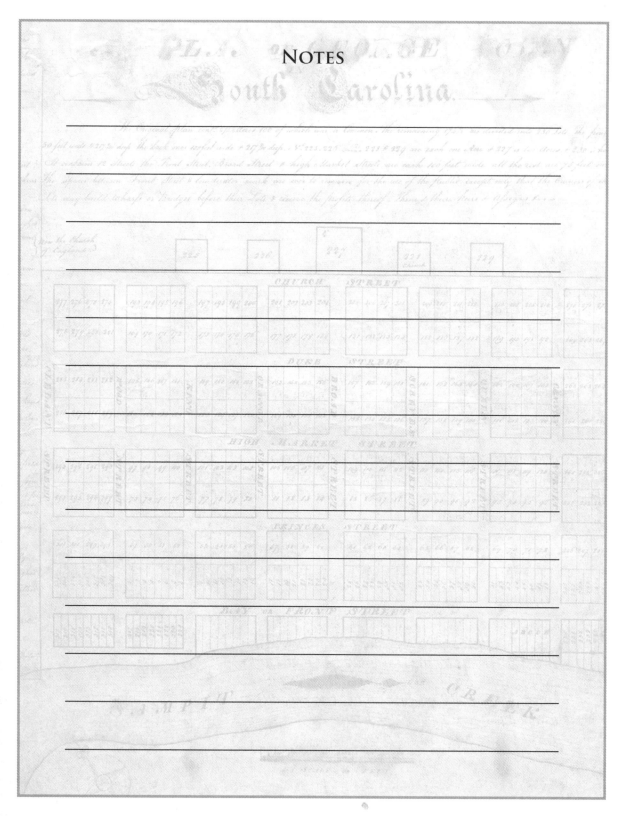

SOUPS, SANDWICHES, SALADS

Independent Seafood and The Red Store Warehouse

Harbor House
Artist: Jean Hanna

Independent Seafood and the Red Store Warehouse are located on the wharf-end of Cannon Street in Georgetown. On the earliest town plan extant, the land on which they now stand was reserved for a fort. In 1753, this lot and adjoining two lots were sold by John Cleland to Benjamin Darling, shipwright. It is likely Mr. Darling used it for a shipyard. Between 1734 and 1774, thirty-three ships were built in and around Georgetown, with Benjamin Darling being the principal builder. In the later part of the eighteenth century, this warehouse was built by a wealthy Huguenot; its construction and bricks attest to that period. In addition to the warehouse, there was a large three-story brick tavern that stood on the corner. The foundation of this may be seen today. This, in its time, was the most fashionable inn in Georgetown. The warehouse was called the "Red Store" (so mentioned in a 1911 deed of conveyance) and the inn, "The French Tavern" or "The Oak Tavern".

The Red Store had one of the largest wharves in town. It was able to accommodate as many as five ships at a time. At this site, the packet ship PATRIOT was docked before leaving on its last mysterious voyage carrying Theodosia Burr Alston, wife of Governor Joseph Alston of South Carolina and daughter of former Vice President Aaron Burr, to an unknown death in 1812.

It is presently used for storage for the adjacent Independent Seafood Company.

BLISSFUL CRAB BISQUE
INDEPENDENT SEAFOOD, GEORGETOWN, SC

½	cup butter	¼	teaspoon celery salt
1	medium onion, finely chopped	⅛	teaspoon white pepper
1	medium carrot, finely chopped	1	quart light cream or milk
2	tablespoons all-purpose flour	8-16	ounces lump crabmeat
1	teaspoon seafood seasoning	3	tablespoons dry white wine
		1	tablespoon snipped parsley
			Salt to taste
			Ground red pepper

Melt butter in a 3 quart saucepan. Add onion and carrot. Cook until tender. Stir in flour, seafood seasoning, celery salt, and white pepper. Gradually add cream, stirring constantly. Stir in crabmeat, wine, parsley, and salt. Simmer 15 to 20 minutes. Do not boil. Sprinkle each serving with dash of ground red pepper. Serve hot.

Yield: 6 servings.

REVELATION 3:20
Here I am! I stand at the door and knock. If anyone hears my voice and opens the door, I will come in and eat with him, and he with me.

COLD CUCUMBER SOUP

5	cucumbers, peeled, seeded, and diced	1½	cups chicken broth (fresh, canned, or bouillon)
1	medium onion, chopped	2	tablespoons butter
2	tablespoons chopped celery leaves	2	tablespoons flour
2	tablespoons chopped parsley	1½	cups half-and-half
1½	teaspoons salt		Parsley, chives, or cucumber for garnish

Simmer cucumbers and next 5 ingredients in a saucepan for 30 minutes. Melt butter in another saucepan and blend in flour; add half-and-half and beat with a wire whisk, stir until thick, and set aside. Purée cucumber mixture in food processor and slowly add to sauce; stir until well blended. Refrigerate overnight. Garnish with parsley, chives, or a slice of cucumber.

Yield: 6 servings.

[handwritten marginal notes:] (½ c hot milk / ½ c milk) basil, grd walnuts (¼ c) drops Tabasco, seasone ½ o. Puree basil + grd walnuts in soup - (garnish w/ basil + toasted grd walnuts)

COLD GREEN SUMMER SOUP

5	cups chicken broth	1	cup chopped celery
2	cups chopped green beans	½	cup chopped scallions
2	cups chopped Romaine lettuce		Salt and pepper to taste
2	cups chopped raw zucchini	¼	cup chopped parsley
1	(10 ounce) box frozen green peas		Sour cream for garnish

Combine all ingredients except parsley and sour cream in a large saucepan. Simmer until tender. Using a blender, blend one cup at a time until smooth. Mix all blended ingredients together and chill for several hours before serving. Add salt and pepper to taste. Garnish with parsley and sour cream prior to serving.

Yield: 10-12 servings.

VICHYSSOISE

2 cups diced potatoes

2 cups diced onions

1 cup chicken broth (canned or fresh)

1 cup sour cream

Salt

Worcestershire sauce to taste

Chopped chives

Cook potatoes and onions in just enough water to cover and until very soft. Put through a fine strainer or food mill. Add chicken broth and let cool. Add sour cream, beat well, season with salt and Worcestershire sauce. Serve in individual bowls. Top with chopped chives.

Yield: 4 servings.

Best cold, but fine hot if a fall rain comes up.

Ruth Long

GAZPACHO

1	large onion, finely chopped	1	teaspoon salt
2	ribs celery, finely chopped	1	teaspoon sugar
2	cucumbers, peeled, seeded, and finely chopped	1	green pepper, finely chopped
1	large tomato, chopped and seeded	2	cloves garlic, minced
8	cups tomato-vegetable juice cocktail	2	tablespoons finely chopped parsley
6	tablespoons salad oil	¼	teaspoon black pepper
4	tablespoons wine vinegar	1	teaspoon Worcestershire sauce
			Hot sauce as desired

Purée onion and celery in food processor. Combine with remaining ingredients in a large jar. Mix well and refrigerate. Keeps well for weeks.

Yield: 8-10 servings.

CREAM OF ARTICHOKE SOUP

1   (14 ounce) can artichoke hearts
2   tablespoons chopped onion
4   tablespoons butter
2   tablespoons flour
1   cup cold milk or half-and-half
1   (14½ ounce) can chicken broth
1   teaspoon lemon juice
    Salt and pepper

Drain and chop artichokes, reserving liquid. Sauté onion in butter until transparent. With wire whisk, stir in flour, then milk or half-and-half until smooth. Add reserved artichoke liquid and chicken broth. Bring to boil. Lower heat to medium. Add lemon juice and artichokes. Season with salt and pepper. Simmer 10 minutes more before serving.

Yield: 4-6 servings.

BLACK BEAN SOUP

CAFE LATTE, CALABASH, NC

½   pound dried black beans
2½ quarts chicken stock
4   slices applewood smoked bacon
1   large onion, finely chopped
1   medium green bell pepper, finely chopped
2   ribs celery, finely chopped
2   teaspoons salt
½   teaspoon pepper
½   teaspoon oregano
6   ounces tomatoes, crushed
    Sour cream and chives for garnish

Wash beans and soak overnight in cold water. Drain beans; cook in stock 1 hour. While beans are cooking, fry bacon in Dutch oven and drain off all but 1 tablespoon of the fat. Add onion, pepper, and celery to the Dutch oven; sauté until lightly browned. Add beans and stock, salt, pepper, oregano, and tomatoes; simmer over medium heat 15 minutes. Garnish each serving with sour cream and chives.

Yield: 8-10 servings.

NOTES

CREAMY ITALIAN WHITE BEAN SOUP

1	tablespoon vegetable oil	¼	teaspoon coarsely ground black pepper
1	medium onion, finely chopped	⅛	teaspoon dried thyme leaves
1	medium celery stalk, finely chopped	2	cups water
1	garlic clove, minced	1	bunch (10-12 ounces) spinach
2	cans (15½ to 19 ounces each) white kidney beans (cannellini)	1	tablespoon fresh lemon juice
1	(10¾ ounce) can chicken broth		Freshly grated Parmesan cheese (optional)

In a 3-quart saucepan, heat oil over medium heat until hot. Add onion and celery and cook 5 to 8 minutes, until tender, stirring occasionally. Add garlic; cook 30 seconds, continue stirring. Rinse and drain beans. Add beans, chicken broth, pepper, thyme, and 2 cups water; heat to boiling over high heat. Reduce heat to low; simmer, uncovered, 15 minutes.

Meanwhile, discard tough stems from spinach; thinly slice leaves.

With a slotted spoon, remove 2 cups bean-vegetable mixture from soup; set aside. In blender at low speed, with center part of cover removed to allow steam to escape, blend remaining soup in small batches until smooth. Pour soup into a large bowl after each batch. Return soup to saucepan; stir in reserved beans and vegetables. Bring to boil over high heat, stirring occasionally. Stir in spinach and cook 1 minute or until wilted. Stir in lemon juice and remove from heat. Serve with Parmesan cheese if you like.

Yield: About 6 cups or 4 main-dish servings.

COME *Lord Jesus, be our guest and in our hearts Your spirit rest. Amen.*

BEEF PICADILLO

½ cup hot beef broth
½ cup golden raisins or currants
1 pound ground beef
½ cup chopped onion
1 clove garlic, finely chopped
1 tablespoon vinegar
¹⁄₁₆ teaspoon of ground cloves

¹⁄₁₆ teaspoon of ground nutmeg
Salt and pepper to taste
1-2 small hot peppers
1 (28 ounce) can whole tomatoes, chopped
½ cup sliced almonds
Prepared rice

Heat broth and pour over raisins soaking them until raisins are plump (about 10 minutes). In a large skillet over medium heat brown ground beef. Add chopped onion and garlic. Reduce heat and cook for 5 minutes. Add raisins with stock, vinegar, cloves, nutmeg, salt, pepper, hot peppers, and tomatoes, breaking them into small pieces. Cook all together for 15 minutes. Add sliced almonds just prior to serving. Serve in bowls over cooked rice.

Yield: 4 servings.

CREAM OF BROCCOLI SOUP

1 pound fresh broccoli florets
½ cup chopped onions
3 tablespoons butter
½ cup flour
6 cups chicken broth

3 cups finely chopped fresh broccoli stalks
2 bay leaves
1 cup evaporated milk
½ teaspoon black pepper, optional

Steam broccoli florets until tender crisp. Drain and set aside. Sauté onion in butter until tender. Add flour, stirring well. Slowly add chicken broth. Gradually stir in chopped broccoli stalks and bay leaves. Cook over medium heat until broccoli is tender. Stir frequently. Remove bay leaves. Purée cooked mixture with submersible wand blender or transfer small amounts to blender and blend until mixture is smooth. Stir in steamed broccoli florets, milk, and optional black pepper.

Yield: 8-10 (1-cup) servings.

This freezes very well.

CARROT AND PARSNIP SOUP

4	onions, chopped	8	cups canned chicken broth
4	boiling potatoes, peeled and diced	8	tablespoons heavy cream
8	carrots, diced		Salt and pepper to taste
8	parsnips, diced	1	teaspoon dried dill weed
8	tablespoons unsalted butter		Sour cream to top

In a saucepan, cook the onions, potatoes, carrots, and parsnips in butter. Cover and cook over moderately low heat for 10 minutes, stirring occasionally. Add the broth and simmer the mixture, covered, for 10 to 15 minutes, stirring occasionally until the vegetables are tender. Purée the mixture in a blender or food processor in batches. Add the cream, dill, salt, and pepper. Cook over moderate heat until hot. Ladle into heated bowls and top with sour cream.

Yield: 12-16 servings.

RANCH CHILI

2	pounds ground beef	2	teaspoons chili powder
1	cup chopped onion	1	teaspoon cumin
1	(28 ounce) can whole tomatoes	1	teaspoon salt
1	(8 ounce) can tomato sauce	1	teaspoon pepper
1	(10 ounce) can tomatoes with chilies	2	(15½ ounce) cans ranch-style beans

Brown beef with onion. Drain. In Dutch oven, place beef and onion. Add can of tomatoes with liquid, mashing and cutting tomatoes into smaller pieces. Add tomato sauce and seasoned tomatoes, and then seasonings. Stir well. Add both cans of ranch-style beans with liquid and stir. Bring to low boil and then simmer, stirring occasionally, until flavors are well-blended, approximately 1 hour.

Yield: 8-10 servings.

Serve with breadsticks or crackers.

CHICKEN TARRAGON SOUP

½	cup chopped celery	1	tablespoon tarragon leaves, dried and crumbled
½	cup chopped onion		
¼	cup butter	1	cup cooked rice
⅓	cup flour	1	cup cooked chicken, diced
5	cups chicken broth		Salt and pepper to taste
3	cups light cream		

Sauté celery and onion in butter over low heat until transparent; blend in flour and cook 3 minutes. Stir in chicken broth, cream, and tarragon. Cook over low heat 15 minutes, stirring occasionally. DO NOT allow mixture to boil. Add rice and chicken to soup. Heat 5 minutes. Add salt and pepper to taste.

Yield: 2½ quarts.

CHICKEN CORN CHOWDER

3	strips bacon, diced	2	medium potatoes, peeled and chopped
½	cup diced celery		
½	cup diced onion	1	(20 ounce) package frozen cream style corn, thawed
½	cup diced carrot		
3	tablespoons all-purpose flour	1	cup whole kernel corn, fresh or frozen
4	cups chicken stock or broth, undiluted and heated	½	teaspoon poultry seasoning
		1	cup heavy cream
2	cups cooked and chopped chicken		Salt and pepper to taste

In a Dutch oven, cook bacon over medium-high heat until crisp. Remove bacon and reserve for garnish. Pour off drippings, reserving 1 tablespoon of drippings in Dutch oven. Add the celery, onion, and carrot to the Dutch oven and cook over medium-high heat until vegetables are tender, stirring frequently. Stir in flour. Cook 3 minutes, stirring constantly. Slowly add stock or broth, stirring constantly with a whisk and scraping sides of pan. Add the chicken, potatoes, corn, and poultry seasoning to vegetable mixture. Cook 10 minutes or until potatoes are tender. Stir in the heavy cream. Cook 3 minutes or until heated through. DO NOT allow mixture to boil. Add salt and pepper. Serve and garnish with cooked, crumbled bacon.

Yield: 8 cups.

NOTES

CHICKEN AND WILD RICE SOUP

1½	cups prepared wild rice	½	cup chopped onion
2	chicken breasts, skinless, boneless	½	cup chopped bell pepper
3	cups low-sodium chicken broth	3	tablespoons flour
1	cup water	1	teaspoon salt
2	tablespoons butter	½	teaspoon pepper
1	cup sliced celery	1	cup half-and-half
½	cup coarsely shredded carrot	⅓	cup sliced almonds, toasted
		¼	cup chopped parsley

Prepare rice according to package directions. Meanwhile, in a large pot, cover chicken with broth, and water; bring to a simmer. Cook for about 10 minutes or until chicken is thoroughly cooked. Skim off any scum that appears on the surface and discard. Remove chicken from broth, let cool slightly; then cut into bite-size cubes. Reserve broth.

In a stockpot, melt butter. Add celery, carrot, onion, and bell pepper; cook until softened, about 5 minutes. Stir in flour, salt, and pepper until slightly thickened. Add wild rice, chicken, reserved broth; stir to combine. Bring to a boil; cover and reduce to a simmer. Cook for 15 minutes, stirring occasionally. Add half-and-half, almonds, and parsley. Cook until just hot. Do not boil.

Yield: 6 servings.

Two tablespoons (or to taste) of sherry may be added just before serving. May be made ahead of time, refrigerated, reheated.

DO NOT *forget to entertain strangers, for by so doing, some people have entertained angels without knowing it.*
Hebrews 13:2

BUBBIE'S SHRIMP AND CORN CHOWDER

1	pound bacon	2	bay leaves
2	large onions, chopped	1	tablespoon basil
3	large potatoes, peeled and cubed	1	quart half-and-half
4-5	cloves garlic, minced	1	pound Polish or other sausage, sliced
1	teaspoon salt	4	tablespoons butter
1	teaspoon pepper	2	pounds raw shrimp, peeled and deveined
2	(14¾ ounce) cans cream-style corn		Salt and pepper to taste
2	(15¼ ounce) cans yellow whole kernel corn		

In a very large heavy bottom pot, fry bacon, crumble, and reserve. Remove half the drippings and add onions. Sauté until translucent. Add cubed potatoes and just enough water to keep potatoes from sticking. Add 4 or 5 cloves of minced garlic, salt, and pepper. Cook on low-medium heat until potatoes are almost done - about 15 minutes. Add corn, bay leaves, basil, and crumbled bacon. Add half-and-half and heat slowly. Lightly brown sausage in a frying pan and add to the pot. Simmer at least 30 minutes or until potatoes are soft. Add salt and pepper to taste. In the last 5 minutes, melt butter in frying pan, sauté shrimp, and add to pot. Remove bay leaves.

Yield: 10 servings.

Buy extra half-and-half to adjust liquid to your personal preference. Whole milk may be used instead of half-and-half. White corn may be used as well as yellow corn. Amount of ingredients is not critical. It is critical that this be made well ahead of time in order to allow the flavors to marry.

B L E S S E D *are those who hunger and thirst for righteousness for they will be filled. Matthew 5:6*

CHEDDAR CHEESE LEEK SOUP

1	bay leaf	4	tablespoons flour
1	teaspoon dried thyme	1½	quarts chicken stock
1	teaspoon peppercorns	1	pound shredded Cheddar cheese
2	tablespoons butter		
⅔	cup finely chopped onion	¾	cup white wine
⅔	cup finely chopped celery	¾	cup half-and-half
⅔	cup finely chopped carrots		Fresh parsley sprigs
2	cups finely chopped leeks		

Prepare bouquet garni: enclose in cheesecloth bay leaf, thyme and peppercorns. In large pot melt butter. Add onion, celery, carrots, and leeks. Sauté until onions are transparent. Blend in flour. Gradually add chicken stock and then immerse bouquet garni in the soup. Bring to boil; simmer for 25 minutes. Remove bouquet garni. Mix and stir in cheese. After cheese has melted, add wine and half-and-half. Stir constantly until soup is well blended. Serve in hot soup bowls; and garnish with parsley.

Yield: 8 servings.

CHEDDAR POTATO SOUP

⅓	cup chopped onion	2	cups (8 ounces) shredded Cheddar cheese
⅓	cup chopped celery		
2	tablespoons butter	2	cups milk
4	cups peeled, diced potatoes	¼	teaspoon pepper
		⅛	teaspoon paprika
3	cups chicken broth		Seasoned croutons
			Minced fresh parsley

In a large saucepan, sauté onion and celery in butter until tender. Add potatoes and broth. Bring to a boil. Reduce heat; cover and simmer for 10-15 minutes or until potatoes are tender. Purée in small batches in a blender until smooth, returning mixture to pan. Stir in cheese, milk, pepper, and paprika. Cook and stir over low heat until the cheese is melted. Garnish with croutons and parsley.

Yield: 8 servings.

LOWCOUNTRY CLAM CHOWDER

12-18	large clams	1	cup chopped onion
2-3	slices of lean fat-back bacon with rind	1	(14 ounce) can chicken broth
1	(7 ounce) package frozen hash brown potatoes		Ketchup
			Hot pepper sauce

Wash clams well and freeze them for a couple of hours to open them and to preserve the clam juice. Chop the bacon into small pieces. Fry them out in a little oil in a large pot. Remove the bacon when crisp and drain. Retain the pan drippings. Sauté the onions in drippings until soft. Add chicken broth to the pot and a few shakes of ketchup. Let simmer. Shuck the clams, preserving as much juice as possible. Cut the clams into small pieces with kitchen shears or chop in food processor. Add them to the pot with as many of the potatoes as you want. Simmer until clams and potatoes are done. Add extra chicken broth or bottled clam juice to stretch. If desired, add the bacon. A few shakes of hot pepper sauce or a little lemon juice perks it up.

Yield: 4-6 servings.

SHE CRAB SOUP IN CREAM

CHIVE BLOSSOM CAFE, PAWLEYS ISLAND, SC

3	large onions, finely diced	7	quarts heavy whipping cream
2½	cups butter, divided use	2	pounds lump crabmeat, picked over
3	cups sherry	3	cups flour
1	quart seafood stock		

Sauté onions in ½ cup butter until tender. Add sherry and reduce for 10 minutes. Add seafood stock. Reduce 5 minutes. Add heavy cream and crabmeat. In separate saucepan melt 2 cups butter. Whisk in 3 cups flour, gradually breaking up any lumps. Slowly whisk flour and butter mixture into soup and bring to a boil. Reduce heat, continue to whisk until thickened and heated through.

Yield: 30-35 servings.

CRAB SOUP

2 tablespoons butter
2 tablespoons flour
2 cups milk
1 cup cream
1 pound crabmeat
Salt and pepper to taste
Sherry to taste (optional)

Melt butter in sauce pan. Remove from heat and add flour blending together well. Slowly add milk while stirring constantly. Return to medium heat and stir until thick. Add cream and crab. Add salt and pepper to taste. Add sherry, if desired.

Yield: 6 servings.

MUSHROOM VEGETABLE CHOWDER

2	pounds fresh mushrooms, sliced	2	(32 ounce) cartons chicken broth
2	large onions, chopped	1	(24 ounce) package frozen broccoli cuts, thawed
¾	cup butter		
¾	cup all-purpose flour	1	(12 ounce) package frozen corn, thawed
1	tablespoon salt		
1	teaspoon pepper	2	cups shredded Cheddar cheese (1 pound)
6	cups milk		

In a large soup kettle or Dutch oven, sauté mushrooms and onions in butter until tender. Combine the flour, salt, and pepper; stir into mushroom mixture until well blended. Gradually stir in milk. Cook and stir until mixture comes to a boil. Cook 2 minutes longer or until thickened and bubbly. Stir in broth, broccoli, and corn; heat through. Just before serving, stir in cheese until melted.

Yield: 25 servings (6 quarts).

LENTIL SOUP

¾	pound German sausage	1	cup chopped celery (with some tops)
1	cup chopped cabbage		
1	pound ground beef	½	cup chopped green pepper
1	(46 ounce) can tomato-vegetable juice cocktail		Salt and pepper to taste
		1	teaspoon oregano
4	cups water	1	bay leaf
1	cup lentils		Shake of basil
1	cup diced carrots	2	beef bouillon cubes
1	cup chopped onion		

Slice and brown sausage. Boil cabbage until it is soft; then drain it. Set sausage and cabbage aside. Brown beef in soup kettle; then drain off liquid. Add tomato-vegetable juice and water. Add remaining ingredients. Cook slowly 1 ½ hours. Taste for seasoning. Add cabbage and sausage just before serving. Remove bay leaf.

Yield: 12 servings.

This was served at the luncheon for the bishops' wives at House of Bishops in 1983.

HEARTY EGGPLANT SOUP

1	small unpeeled eggplant	1	(14 ounce) can reduced fat beef broth
1	tablespoon olive oil	½	teaspoon salt
1	tablespoon butter	½	teaspoon sugar
1	small onion, chopped	¼	teaspoon fresh ground pepper
½	pound ground round		
½	green bell pepper, cut into thin strips 2 inches long	¼	teaspoon nutmeg
1	clove garlic, minced	3	tablespoons small pasta
1	small carrot, shredded	3	tablespoons fresh parsley
1	(16 ounce) can whole peeled tomatoes		Dry red wine (optional)
			Grated Parmesan cheese (optional)

Slice and cube eggplant into ¾-inch pieces. Heat oil and butter in Dutch oven. Add onion and cook, stirring until limp. Crumble meat into pot with pepper strips. Stir over medium-to-high heat until meat is no longer pink. Skim off any fat. Add eggplant cubes, garlic, carrot, tomatoes (breaking them up with a spoon) with their liquid, beef broth, salt, sugar, pepper, and nutmeg. Bring to a boil, reduce heat, and simmer (covered) 30 to 45 minutes. Add pasta and parsley. Cover and simmer an additional 10 to 15 minutes. Serve in bowls and splash some red wine on top and sprinkle with fresh, grated Parmesan cheese, if desired.

Yield: 3-6 servings.

SHE CRAB SOUP

1	pound crabmeat	3	(12 ounce) cans evaporated milk
½	cup butter		
⅛	teaspoon mace	2	(10¾ ounce) cans mushroom soup
⅛	teaspoon nutmeg		Sherry to taste

Sauté 1 pound crabmeat in butter. Add mace and nutmeg. Add milk and mushroom soup. Stir until well blended. Allow to cook a short time. Add sherry to taste.

Yield: 10-12 servings.

Add roe from crab with milk.

To extend she crab soup, add 3-4 finely chopped hard-cooked eggs with the milk.

MULLIGATAWNY SOUP

½   cup finely chopped onion
1½ teaspoons curry powder
2   tablespoons vegetable oil
1   tart apple, peeled and chopped
½   cup chopped carrots
½   cup chopped celery
¼   cup chopped green pepper
3   tablespoons flour
4   cups chicken broth

1   (16 ounce) can whole tomatoes, chopped and undrained
1   tablespoon chopped parsley
2   teaspoons lemon juice
1   teaspoon sugar
2   whole cloves
¼   teaspoon salt
⅛   teaspoon pepper
1   cup cooked, diced chicken
    Cooked noodles, optional

Cook onion and curry powder in oil until tender. Stir in apple, carrots, celery, and green pepper. Cook, stirring occasionally, until vegetables are crisp, but tender - about 5 minutes. Sprinkle flour over mixture, stirring to mix well. Gradually add all remaining ingredients except chicken. Bring to a boil; add chicken. Simmer, stirring occasionally, for 30 minutes.

Yield: 8-10 servings or more if noodles are added.

Cooked noodles may be added to make an even heartier soup.

OKRA SOUP

3 strips bacon

½ large onion, finely chopped

2 (14 ounce) cans tomatoes, whole or chopped

Salt and pepper, to taste

1 teaspoon fresh thyme

1 bay leaf

1 pound cut frozen okra

½ cup fresh okra, cut in larger pieces

4 cups beef broth

Hot sauce, to taste

Cooked rice

Cook bacon until crisp; remove bacon. Sauté onion in drippings. Add tomatoes. If whole tomatoes, break into pieces with fork. Add salt, pepper, bay leaf, and thyme. Cook this mixture until thickened. Add okra and beef broth. Allow to simmer until okra is tender, about 15-20 minutes. Add a splash of hot sauce to taste. Remove bay leaf.

Yield: 4 servings.

Serve in bowls with cooked rice and top with crumbled bacon.

FRENCH ONION SOUP

8   onions, thinly sliced
5   tablespoons butter
4   tablespoons flour
2   cloves garlic, crushed
2   teaspoons sugar
⅛   teaspoon parsley
⅛   teaspoon dried thyme

4   (10¾ ounce) cans beef consommé
3½ cups water
2   cups white wine
2   tablespoons brandy
    French bread
    Parmesan cheese
    Mozzarella slices

Sauté onions with butter until golden. Add flour, garlic, and sugar. Stir over medium heat. Add parsley, thyme, beef consommé, water, wine, and brandy. Simmer 45 minutes. Place slices of French bread in ovenproof soup bowls. Sprinkle with Parmesan cheese and fill bowls with soup. Cover with thick slice of mozzarella cheese and melt under broiler.

Yield: 8 servings.

OYSTER STEW

3	dozen fresh raw oysters	3	tablespoons all-purpose flour
7	tablespoons unsalted butter	5	cups heated milk
1	medium onion, finely diced (about 1 cup)	2	cups heated heavy cream
1	stalk celery, finely diced (optional)		Salt to taste
			Fresh ground pepper
		1/16	teaspoon cayenne pepper

Shuck oysters. Place them in a bowl and save their liquor in another bowl. Melt the butter in a saucepan. Add onion and celery and heat through until translucent - about 10 minutes. Add flour, stirring constantly for 2 minutes. Gradually add heated milk, cream, and oyster liquor. Heat well on low heat. Add salt and peppers. Add oysters just before serving. Allow edges of oysters to curl.

Yield: 6-8 servings.

Do not overcook oysters as they will become tough.

OYSTER SOUP

1	pint oysters with their liquor	2	cups milk
		1	teaspoon salt
3	tablespoons butter	1/4	teaspoon pepper
1/2	cup finely chopped celery	1	cup light cream
1/4	cup finely chopped onion	2	tablespoons fresh chopped parsley
1/4	cup finely chopped carrot		
3	tablespoons flour		

Drain oysters and reserve the liquor. Heat butter in saucepan. Add celery, onion, and carrots and cook over medium heat for 3 minutes. Sprinkle in flour and stir to blend. Cook for 2 minutes. Add oyster liquor to vegetables, stirring constantly. Stir in milk and seasonings. Simmer gently until vegetables are tender. Add oysters and return to a simmer (DO NOT BOIL). Add cream and serve. Sprinkle each serving with fresh parsley.

Yield: 6 servings.

Spring onion can be substituted for whole onion.

North Inlet oysters are preferable. If used, do not use additional salt.

NOTES

CREAM OF PARSLEY SOUP WITH OYSTERS AND BACON

¼ pound sliced smoked bacon

2 tablespoons unsalted butter

2 large shallots, minced

½ cup dry white wine

12 freshly shucked oysters, liquid reserved

2 cups chicken stock

1 medium Idaho potato, peeled and diced

3 cups parsley, large stems removed (about 2 bunches)

1 cup milk

½ cup heavy cream

¼ teaspoon salt

1 teaspoon freshly ground pepper

Sprigs of parsley for garnish

In a large skillet, cook the bacon over moderate heat until crisp. Drain on paper towel and cut into 1-inch pieces. In a large saucepan, melt the butter over low heat. Add the shallots and sauté until soft but not brown, about 5 minutes. Increase the heat to high and add the wine, reserved oyster liquid, chicken stock, and potato. Bring to boil; reduce heat to low. Simmer until the potato is tender, about 8 minutes. Add the parsley and cook until soft, about 3 minutes. Transfer the mixture to a blender and purée until smooth. Pour the soup back into the saucepan. Add the milk and cream and reheat over moderate heat. Add the oysters and cook for 1 minute. Season with salt and pepper. Ladle the soup into bowls and garnish with the reserved bacon and parsley springs.

Yield: 4 servings.

This rich soup can be prepared two days ahead up to the point of adding the oysters. Serve it as a first course or with salad as a light lunch.

I AM *the vine and my Father is the gardener. He cuts off every branch in me that bears no fruit, while every branch that does bear fruit, He prunes so that it will be even more fruitful. John 15:1,2*

ITALIAN PEA SOUP

2	cups dried green split peas	1	bay leaf
2	quarts water	¼	cup fresh parsley or
1	cup sliced celery		⅛ cup dried parsley
½	cup diced onion	½	teaspoon basil
1	cup sliced carrots	½	teaspoon oregano
1	cup diced potato	1	teaspoon Italian seasoning
1	clove garlic, minced	1	teaspoon salt
		¹⁄₁₆	teaspoon cayenne pepper

Put all ingredients in a large pot. Cook for 2 hours, stirring occasionally. Remove bay leaf before serving.

Yield: 6-8 servings.

This recipe can be doubled or tripled.

POSOLE

(PRONOUNCED PO-SO-LAY)

MEXICAN BEEF AND HOMINY SOUP

4	cups dried pinto beans	1-2	tablespoons dried oregano
2	pieces beef shank, bone-in	1	(15½ ounce) can hominy,
5	quarts water		drained
4	bay leaves	3	beef bouillon cubes
2	tablespoons onion powder		Salt
10	cloves garlic, peeled,		Cilantro, fresh and
	ends trimmed		chopped for garnish
	(very important!)		Crushed red pepper

Sort and wash beans. Add beans to stockpot with beef, water, bay leaves, onion powder, garlic cloves, and oregano. Bring to boil. Reduce heat to low; simmer 3 hours. Remove bones and meat. Set aside to cool. Add hominy. Cook another 20 minutes or so. Pull meat from bones. Remove bay leaves. Taste. Add bouillon cubes and salt to taste. Add meat. Heat thoroughly. Spoon into bowls; top with cilantro and red pepper, to taste.

Yield: 8 servings.

SPLIT GREEN PEA SOUP

2 cups split green peas

1 ham hock with meat

10 cups water

2 chopped carrots

2 chopped onions

2 stalks celery, chopped

Soak peas overnight in water to cover. Strain, add 10 cups water, vegetables, and ham hock. Cook several hours, remove meat, and put soup in blender. Add salt and pepper to taste and milk if too thick. Put meat into soup.

Yield:8-10 servings.

Emily Bull

PUMPKIN SOUP

¼	cup butter	⅛	teaspoon ginger
2	small celery stalks, chopped	⅛	teaspoon nutmeg
⅓	cup chopped onion	⅛	teaspoon cloves
2	cloves garlic, minced	½	teaspoon salt
3	cups chicken broth, divided use	⅛	teaspoon cayenne
		1	(15 ounce) can pumpkin
		1	cup half-and-half

Melt butter and sauté celery, onions, and garlic. Mix in blender with one cup of chicken broth. Add seasonings. Put this mixture in a large saucepan. Add pumpkin and remaining broth. Cook on medium heat until hot. Add half-and-half. Do not boil.

Yield: 6 servings.

NORTHWEST SALMON CHOWDER

3	tablespoons butter	½	teaspoon pepper
½	cup chopped celery	¼-¾	teaspoon dill weed
½	cup chopped onion	1	(14¾ ounce) can cream style corn
½	cup chopped green pepper	2	cups half-and-half
1	garlic clove, minced	1¾-2	cups fully cooked salmon chunks OR 1 (14¾ ounce) can salmon, drained, flaked, bones and skin removed
1	(14½ ounce) can chicken broth		
1	cup uncooked potatoes, peeled and diced		
1	cup shredded carrots		
1½	teaspoons salt		

In a large saucepan, sauté celery, onion, green pepper, and garlic in butter until the vegetables are tender. Add broth, potatoes, carrots, salt, pepper, and dill. Bring to boil. Reduce heat. Cover and simmer for 30 minutes or until vegetables are nearly tender. Stir in corn, cream, and salmon. Simmer for 15 minutes or until heated through.

Yield: 8 servings.

Shrimp and Artichoke Soup

1 (24 ounce) can artichokes, drained
1 quart chicken broth
2 cups chopped green onions (separated into 1 cup each)
Salt to taste
Creole seasoning, to taste

1 tablespoon crushed dried thyme or dried rosemary
¼ cup melted butter
¼ cup + 1 tablespoon flour
1 quart heavy cream
½-1 pound shrimp, peeled and deveined
1 tablespoon chopped parsley (to garnish)

Combine artichokes, chicken stock, 1 cup green onions, salt, Creole seasoning, and thyme. Bring mixture to a boil. Reduce heat and simmer for about 12-15 minutes. In a small saucepan combine butter and flour to make a light roux. Add roux to the simmering pot. Stir in heavy cream and simmer for 10 minutes or until thickened. Salt to taste. Add shrimp and simmer for 5 minutes. Serve with 1 cup chopped green onions and parsley to garnish.

Yield: 6-8 servings.

Taco Soup

1 pound ground beef, browned
1 envelope taco seasoning
1 envelope dry Ranch dressing mix
2 cups water
1 (15 ounce) can shoepeg corn
1 (16 ounce) can pinto beans

1 (15 ounce) can black beans
1 (15½ ounce) can chili beans
2 (14½ ounce) cans diced tomatoes
Shredded Cheddar cheese
Sour cream

Mix all together except cheese and sour cream. Bring to low boil; simmer for 45 minutes. Ladle into serving bowls; top with shredded Cheddar cheese and dollops of sour cream. Serve with tortilla chips.

Yield: 4-6 servings.

For variation add 1 teaspoon sugar, 1 teaspoon cumin, and 1 teaspoon fresh cilantro.

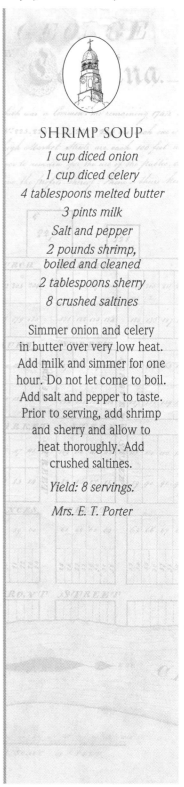

SHRIMP SOUP

1 cup diced onion

1 cup diced celery

4 tablespoons melted butter

3 pints milk

Salt and pepper

2 pounds shrimp, boiled and cleaned

2 tablespoons sherry

8 crushed saltines

Simmer onion and celery in butter over very low heat. Add milk and simmer for one hour. Do not let come to boil. Add salt and pepper to taste. Prior to serving, add shrimp and sherry and allow to heat thoroughly. Add crushed saltines.

Yield: 8 servings.

Mrs. E. T. Porter

SAUSAGE, SHRIMP, AND CORN CHOWDER

1	cup chopped beef sausage	1	cup half-and-half
¼	cup chopped onion	1	cup milk
¼	cup chopped celery	1	(15 ounce) can shoepeg or white corn
2	tablespoons bacon drippings or butter	½	teaspoon seafood seasoning
1	(3 ounce) package cream cheese	3	bay leaves
1	(10¾ ounce) can cream of potato soup		Salt and pepper to taste
		1½	pounds raw shrimp, peeled and cleaned

Boil sausage according to package directions. Sauté onion and celery in drippings or butter. In a large pot, combine sausage pieces, onion, and celery. Add cream cheese, stirring until melted. Add soup, half-and-half, milk, corn, and spices. Simmer until hot. Add shrimp. Cook until shrimp are pink. Remove bay leaves. Serve with cornbread.

Yield: 7-8 servings.

Lower calorie substitution for half-and-half and milk: ½ cup fat free half-and-half and 1½ cups skim milk.

To reheat, add ½ cup milk.

Old Bay Seasoning was recommended in this recipe.

TOMATO BASIL SOUP

ROZ'S RICE MILL CAFE, PAWLEYS ISLAND, SC

1	(16 ounce) can whole tomatoes, drained and crushed	1	teaspoon minced garlic
		1	teaspoon dried oregano
		1	teaspoon dried thyme
1	(22 ounce) can cream of celery soup	2	teaspoons dried basil
		1	cup sour cream
1	(22 ounce) can cream of potato soup	1	quart half-and-half (or milk)

Combine all ingredients in large saucepan. Cook slowly on medium-low heat until hot.

Yield: 6-8 servings.

Purée and chill to serve as a cold soup.

If using fresh herbs, add them when soup is hot.

FRIED TOMATO SOUP

OROBOSA'S LOWCOUNTRY CAFE, PAWLEYS ISLAND, SC

3	tablespoons olive oil	1	quart chicken or seafood stock
½	cup chopped sweet onion		
5	ounces tomato paste	1	teaspoon chopped thyme
4	tomatoes, peeled and chopped	1	teaspoon basil
			Basil for garnish
1½	teaspoons garlic		Salt and pepper, to taste

Put oil in saucepan and heat to medium. Add onion and sauté until fragrant. Add tomato paste and blend for 5 minutes, until tomato paste turns from red to dark brown. Add fresh tomatoes and simmer 2 minutes. Add garlic and stock and bring to simmer; simmer 2 minutes. Add thyme, basil, salt, and pepper. Bring to simmer and then serve garnished with chopped basil.

Yield: 4-6 servings.

Can also be served with wilted spinach in it, and/or with a 2-ounce portion of grilled grouper placed in the middle of the soup bowl.

TOMATO PEPPER CREAM SOUP

2	tablespoons oil		Salt, pepper to taste
2	medium green bell peppers, cut in thin strips		Hot pepper sauce to taste
		1	(12 ounce) can evaporated milk
1	(14 ounce) can whole tomatoes, drained and diced		
		¼	pound Monterey Jack cheese, grated
1	(10¾ ounce) can chicken broth		

Heat oil. Sauté peppers until almost limp; then add tomatoes. Add broth and simmer uncovered for about 10 minutes to reduce by about half. Stir in seasonings. Reduce heat to lowest setting. Add milk. When ready to serve, add cheese and heat very gently until cheese is melted. Do not boil or overcook at this stage or it will curdle.

Yield: 4 servings.

Green bell peppers can be substituted with one red and one yellow pepper. You may also substitute 3 fresh tomatoes, peeled, seeded, and diced if you prefer. You may fully or partially purée the soup with an immersion blender before the addition of the cheese if you do not like bits and pieces in your soup.

TORTELLINI SOUP

3 tablespoons butter

1 medium onion, chopped

3-4 cloves garlic, minced

1 package frozen chopped spinach, unthawed

1 (14 ounce) can diced tomatoes

3 (10¾ ounce) cans chicken broth

1 package dried cheese tortellini

Melt butter in stockpot. Sauté onion and garlic. Add spinach and tomatoes. Continue to cook for 5 minutes. Add chicken broth. Cook for 10 minutes. Add tortellini. Cover. Soup is ready to serve when tortellini are plump. Add more chicken stock, if needed.

Yield: 4-6 servings.

UDON SOUP

Yokoso, North Myrtle Beach, SC

4 cups chicken or vegetable broth

2 cups frozen udon (flat Japanese noodles similar to fettuccine)

Cooked seafood, ground beef, or vegetables

2 green onions, shredded

Bring broth to a boil. Add frozen noodles and reduce heat; cook until noodles are separated. Ladle into four bowls and add hot seafood, beef, or vegetables. Garnish with green onions.

Yield: 4 servings.

Yokoso recommends shrimp tempura for an incredible flavor.

TOMATO-BEAN SOUP WITH PASTA

1	cup acini di pepe or any small soup pasta	1	(28 ounce) can diced tomatoes
2	tablespoons olive or vegetable oil	¼	cup red wine
2	cloves garlic, minced	2	teaspoons Italian herb blend
1	small yellow onion, diced	1	bay leaf, optional
2	(14½ ounce) cans vegetable or chicken broth	1	teaspoon salt
		¼	teaspoon freshly ground pepper
2	(15 ounce) cans cannellini or black beans	4	kale or Swiss chard leaves, coarsely chopped
			Grated Parmesan cheese

Prepare pasta according to package directions. Meanwhile, heat oil in large saucepan over medium heat. Add garlic and onion; cook until fragrant, about 5 minutes. Reduce heat. Add broth, beans with their liquid, tomatoes with their liquid, wine, Italian seasoning, bay leaf, salt and pepper. Simmer 20 minutes. Remove bay leaf. Add chard leaves; cook until slightly wilted, about 5 minutes. Ladle soup into bowls; add pasta. Pass Parmesan cheese at the table.

Yield: 6-8 servings.

Note: Acini di pepe ("peppercorns") are tiny soup pasta; Only tiny pasta will work here.

HE IS *like a tree planted by streams of water, which yields its fruit in season and whose leaf does not wither. Whatever he does prospers. Psalm 1:3*

HEARTY VEGETABLE SOUP

1	pound breakfast sausage roll (mild or spicy)
1	large onion, chopped
1	clove garlic, minced
2	ribs celery, sliced
1	(10 ounce) can diced tomatoes
1	potato, peeled and cubed
1	(16 ounce) bag frozen mixed vegetables

½ cup frozen lima beans (if not included in mixed vegetables)
4 (10¾ ounce) cans chicken broth
1 tablespoon Worcestershire sauce
1 tablespoon vinegar
1 tablespoon sugar
1 teaspoon Italian seasoning
1 zucchini, sliced
   Grated Parmesan cheese

PROVERBS: 12:11

He who works his land will have abundant food, but he who chases fantasies lacks judgment.

Brown and crumble sausage. Drain on paper towels. In large pot, brown onion and garlic. Add remaining ingredients (except zucchini and Parmesan cheese). If too thick, add more chicken broth. Bring to boil. Reduce heat and cook until vegetables are tender. Add sliced zucchini and cook for a few minutes more. At this point, you may also add leftover vegetables or cooked pasta. Heat through. Adjust seasonings. Serve with Parmesan cheese and Italian bread.

Yield: 8-10 servings.

This keeps well and can be frozen.

ELEGANT WILD RICE SOUP

2	tablespoons butter
¼	cup finely chopped celery
1	tablespoon minced onion
¼	cup flour
4	cups chicken broth
2	cups cooked wild rice
⅓	cup finely grated carrots

½ teaspoon salt
   Freshly ground pepper
1 cup half-and-half
2 tablespoons dry sherry
   Minced parsley
3 tablespoons toasted, chopped, slivered almonds

Melt butter in saucepan. Add onion and celery; sauté until tender. Blend in flour. Add broth and cook, stirring until mixture thickens. Stir in rice, carrots, salt and pepper. Simmer for about 5 minutes. Blend in half-and-half and sherry. Heat to serving temperature. Garnish servings with parsley and almonds.

Yield: 6-7 servings.

May be made ahead: refrigerate, reheat, and garnish.

WINTER SOUP

1	pound lean ground beef	1	tablespoon Worcestershire sauce
1	onion, chopped	½	teaspoon salt
½	large green pepper, chopped	½	teaspoon pepper
1	clove garlic, crushed	½	soup can red wine or water
1	(16 ounce) can tomatoes	1	(15½ ounce) can red kidney beans
1	(8 ounce) can tomato sauce	½	head of cabbage, chopped
1	(10¾ ounce) beef consommé		

Sauté ground beef until brown. Add onion, green pepper, and garlic. Cook 15 minutes. Add all other ingredients except cabbage. Simmer covered for 1 hour. Add cabbage and cook 30 minutes longer.

Yield: 6 servings.

Soup will thicken when lid is removed. This soup freezes well. Pumpernickel toast and a little fruit makes a meal.

CRAB MELT SANDWICH

1	pound crabmeat	4	slices Italian bread, crust removed
2	tablespoons lime juice, divided use		Butter
½	cup mayonnaise	1-2	large tomatoes
2	teaspoons Dijon mustard	4	teaspoons freshly grated Parmesan cheese
	Salt and pepper to taste		

Put crabmeat in a bowl and add 1 tablespoon lime juice and toss. In a small bowl mix together remaining tablespoon lime juice, mayonnaise, and mustard until smooth. Pour sauce over crab and toss to coat. Season with salt and pepper and chill, covered for about 30 minutes. Lightly toast bread on one side; then butter untoasted side. Cut tomatoes into thick slices and place on buttered, untoasted side of bread slices. Spread each sandwich with the topping mixture and sprinkle each with 1 teaspoon Parmesan cheese and broil in a preheated broiler 3-5 inches from heat until cheese is melted.

Yield: 4 servings.

Swiss cheese may be substituted for Parmesan cheese.

ISLAND TACOS

MAHI MAHI FILLETS

½ cup tequila	1 tablespoon hot sauce
¼ cup roughly chopped cilantro	1 tablespoon chili powder
	¼ cup canola oil
Juice of 1 lime	1 pound mahi-mahi fillets

Preheat grill. Combine tequila, cilantro, lime juice, hot sauce, and chili powder. Whisk in canola oil. Put marinade in a zip bag and add the mahi-mahi fillets. Seal bag and let marinade for 30-60 minutes. Put marinated fillets on hot grill. Cook until fillets are firm and remove from grill. Let the fish cool and then flake them with a fork.

TORTILLAS

8 flour tortillas	Sour cream
1 head of napa cabbage, thinly shredded	Salsa
	Guacamole
Hot sauce	

Warm tortillas on the grill. Place a serving of mahi-mahi fillets in a tortilla, top with shredded cabbage, hot sauce, sour cream, salsa, and/or guacamole.

Yield: 6-8 servings.

ITALIAN CHICKEN WRAPS

1 (16 ounce) package stir-fry vegetable blend	½ cup fat-free Italian salad dressing
2 (6 ounce) packages ready-to-serve chicken strips, grilled	3 tablespoons shredded Parmesan cheese
	6 (8 inch) flour tortillas, warmed

In a saucepan, cook vegetables according to package directions; drain. Stir in the chicken, salad dressing, and cheese. Simmer, uncovered, for 3-4 minutes or until heated through. Spoon about ¾ cup down the center of each tortilla; roll up tightly.

Yield: 6 servings.

PLANTATION TOUR'S TURKEY SALAD FOR SANDWICHES

5 fifteen pound turkeys, cooked and diced

9 bunches of celery, diced

10 bottles of capers and juice

1 small bottle hot pepper sauce

1 small bottle seasoned salt

10 quarts mayonnaise

Mix all ingredients into mayonnaise and blend thoroughly. There is enough mayonnaise in the salad so the bread does not have to be spread separately.

Hellmann's mayonnaise was recommended for this recipe.

We have always felt the lunches were a real necessity for our visitors, particularly as it is difficult to find food on both the Santee and the Black/Peedee River tours. Finding delicious food on the Waccamaw Neck has never been a problem. Elsewhere only an occasional country store offering soft drinks and nabs is available.

Yield: 300 sandwiches.

Julia Pyatt Kaminski

PLANTATION TOURS FINGER SANDWICHES

1 (8 ounce) package cream cheese, softened

1 (5¾ ounce) jar green olives, drained and chopped

⅓ cup ground pecans

1½ tablespoons dried onion soup mix

1 rounded tablespoon mayonnaise

Buttermilk white bread, crust removed

Mix and mash first 5 ingredients together. Spread between crustless bread slices. Cut in triangular shapes.

A GOOD CHICKEN OR TURKEY SALAD

2 cups cooked and chopped chicken or turkey

2 cups chopped apples

2 teaspoons lemon juice

2 tablespoons chopped celery

2 tablespoons raisins

Mayonnaise, to taste

Mix ingredients together.

Yield: 4 servings.

Serve on bread for sandwiches or on greens for a salad plate.

VEGETABLE SANDWICHES

2	cucumbers, peeled and grated	1	(¼ ounce) envelope unflavored gelatin
1	small onion, grated	½	cup water, divided use
1	small bell pepper, chopped	2	cups mayonnaise
2	tomatoes, chopped		

Drain vegetables thoroughly. Soften gelatin in ¼ cup cold water in a medium bowl. Add ¼ cup boiling water, stirring until dissolved. Stir vegetables into gelatin. Add mayonnaise to the mixture and stir until blended. Chill in airtight container overnight. Serve as spread on bread or crackers.

CUCUMBER SANDWICHES

Cucumbers, peeled	**White bread**
Italian dressing	**Mayonnaise**

Slice cucumbers and marinate in Italian dressing overnight. Cut circles from bread using a biscuit cutter or small juice glass. Spread mayonnaise on bread. Place cucumber slice on bread.

Duke's Mayonnaise was recommended for this recipe.

SHRIMP PASTE

2	pounds shrimp, peeled		Juice of 1 lemon
	Salt		Hot pepper sauce, to taste
1-2	tablespoons grated onion or onion juice	1½	cups mayonnaise

Cook shrimp in salted water. Drain and grind. Mix all ingredients and let stand overnight. Add more salt and mayonnaise if needed. Serve as sandwich spread or on crackers.

Yield: Makes 18 sandwiches.

Hellmann's mayonnaise was recommended for this recipe.

ALAD WITH
AND PECANS

3	tablespoons chopped fresh parsley
1	tablespoon Dijon mustard
2	celery ribs, chopped
½	small red onion, chopped
¼	teaspoon salt
¼	teaspoon pepper

ll overnight for best flavor.

Yield: 5 cups.

h.

FROZEN CRANBERRY SALAD

1	(8 ounce) package cream cheese	1	(16 ounce) can whole cranberry sauce
2	tablespoons mayonnaise	½	cup chopped walnuts
2	tablespoons sugar	1	(8 ounce) frozen nondairy whipped topping
1	(20 ounce) can crushed pineapple, drained		

Blend first 3 ingredients together. Add remaining ingredients. Pour into a 2-quart casserole dish and freeze.

Yield: 8-10 servings.

VERSATILE CRANBERRIES

As early as the 1500s, cranberries were used as food, dye, and medicine. The tartness of cranberries makes them a good match for sweet fruits, such as apples. Their strong flavor also complements the light taste of white meats. Cranberries have a high vitamin C content and they contain heart-healthy antioxidants. You can find them canned and frozen year-round, but stock up on fresh ones during their peak season, October through December. Once frozen, they're recipe-ready for up to a year.

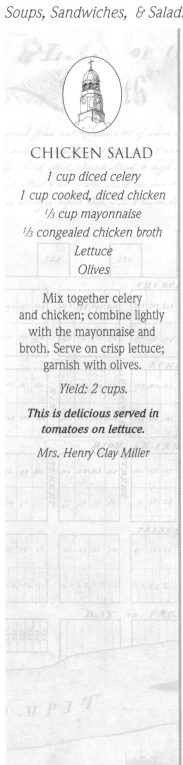

CHICKEN SALAD

1 cup diced celery

1 cup cooked, diced chicken

⅓ cup mayonnaise

⅓ congealed chicken broth

Lettuce

Olives

Mix together celery and chicken; combine lightly with the mayonnaise and broth. Serve on crisp lettuce; garnish with olives.

Yield: 2 cups.

This is delicious served in tomatoes on lettuce.

Mrs. Henry Clay Miller

CRANBERRY SALAD

1	(16 ounce) can whole cranberry sauce
1	(3 ounce) package raspberry gelatin
1	cup boiling water
¼	teaspoon salt
1	tablespoon lemon juice
½	cup mayonnaise
1	apple or orange peeled and diced
½	cup finely chopped pecans

Heat cranberry sauce. Put in colander to drain. Dissolve gelatin in hot cranberry juice and boiling water. Cool in refrigerator until almost set. Sprinkle salt and lemon juice over drained cranberries and apple. Whip in mayonnaise, fold in apple, cranberries, and nuts. Congeal in glass baking dish or mold.

Yield: 6 servings — may be doubled.

Hellmann's Mayonnaise was recommended for this recipe.

APPLE AND HAVARTI QUESADILLA

1	Granny Smith apple, peeled, cored, and thinly sliced
¼	red bell pepper, chopped
3	green onions
3½	tablespoons butter, divided use
¼	teaspoon cayenne pepper
¼	teaspoon salt
2	teaspoons cider vinegar
1	clove garlic, minced
1	teaspoon brown sugar
4	flour tortillas
8	ounces Havarti cheese, thinly sliced
1	large egg, beaten

Preheat broiler. In a skillet over medium heat, sauté apple, bell pepper, and onions in 1 ½ tablespoons butter until soft. Add cayenne pepper, salt, vinegar, garlic, and brown sugar. Heat about 2-3 minutes. Place tortillas on rack in broiler and heat until soft, about 30 seconds. Arrange cheese over half the tortilla, leaving ½-inch border. Top with apple mixture. Brush the edges of the tortilla with egg and fold in half. Press to seal. Melt 2 tablespoons butter in a skillet over medium heat. Cook quesadillas until brown, about 1 ½ minutes per side. Drain on paper towels. Cut and serve warm.

Yield: 4 servings.

GRAPEFRUIT SALAD

1	(¼ ounce) envelope unflavored gelatin	2	grapefruits, peeled and sectioned
½	cup cold water	2	oranges, peeled and sectioned
1	cup boiling water	¾	cup diced celery
¼	cup sugar		Romaine lettuce
¼	teaspoon salt		Poppy seed dressing
¼	cup lemon juice		
	Vegetable cooking spray		

Dissolve gelatin in cold water. Add boiling water, sugar, salt, and lemon juice. Spray small individual molds with a light layer of cooking spray. Arrange fruits and celery in the mold, and cover with gelatin mixture. Chill overnight. Unmold onto a bed of romaine lettuce, and serve with poppy seed dressing.

Yield: 6-8 servings.

LAYERED FRUIT IN LEMON-PEAR SAUCE

1	(29 ounce) can pear halves in heavy syrup	1	(16 ounce) can pineapple chunks, drained
1	egg, beaten	2	bananas, sliced
2	tablespoons flour	1	pint strawberries, sliced
1	teaspoon melted butter	1	(16 ounce) can Mandarin oranges, drained
2	teaspoons lemon juice		
1	cup heavy cream, whipped	2	kiwis
2	tablespoons powdered sugar	¼	cup slivered almonds, toasted

Drain pears, reserving 1 cup of syrup. Combine syrup, egg, and flour. Cook over medium heat until thick. Stir in butter and lemon juice. Cool. Fold in whipped cream that has been sweetened with sugar.

Dice all but 2 pear halves. Layer pears, pineapple, bananas, strawberries, and oranges in a glass bowl. Spread the topping over all and chill overnight. Peel and slice kiwis just before serving. Garnish top with almonds, kiwis, and remaining pear halves.

Yield: 8-10 servings.

POPPY SEED DRESSING OR SAUCE

¾ cup sugar

1 tablespoon dry mustard

1 teaspoon salt

⅓ cup cider vinegar

1 tablespoon onion juice

1 cup salad oil

1 tablespoon poppy seeds

Mix first 4 ingredients. Add onion juice. At medium speed, slowly add oil. Beat until thick. Add poppy seeds. Keep refrigerated. Use it for fruit or over ham.

Yield: 2 cups.

Emily Stacey

*2 medium cucumbers,
peeled and thinly sliced*

1 medium onion, thinly sliced

⅓ cup vinegar

1 tablespoon sugar

1 teaspoon salt

½ teaspoon dried dill weed

⅛ teaspoon cracked pepper

Put all ingredients
in ceramic bowl — not plastic.
Mix and refrigerate.

Yield: 4 servings.

**Wonderful on a
hot summer day.**

SAN FRANCISCO SALAD

3	tablespoons butter	8	ounces lettuce and a little spinach
1	cup broken pecans or walnuts	¾	cup dried cranberries
½	cup sugar	½	pound feta cheese, crumbled
1	tablespoon course ground pepper		

Melt butter in small pan; add nuts and sauté over medium heat for about 5 minutes being careful not to burn. Then mix sugar, coarse ground pepper, and nuts. Stir until sugar is dissolved. In large bowl, toss lettuce, spinach, cranberries, and cheese.

DRESSING

2	teaspoons sugar	¼	teaspoon pepper
1	cup chopped fresh parsley	½	cup red wine vinegar
1	teaspoon dried oregano	4	cloves garlic, finely chopped (optional)
¼	cup chopped onion		
¼	teaspoon salt		

Put all dressing ingredients in blender and mix well. Pour over lettuce mixture; add nuts. Toss well.

Yield: 8 servings.

CUCUMBER-LIME MOUSSE CONGEALED SALAD

1	(3 ounce) package lime gelatin	½	cup mayonnaise
1	cup hot water	2	cups sour cream
2	large cucumbers	½	teaspoon pepper
1	tablespoon lime juice	1	teaspoon salt
1	teaspoon Worcestershire sauce	¼	teaspoon hot pepper sauce

Dissolve gelatin in hot water and chill to consistency of unbeaten egg whites. Peel cucumbers, remove seeds, and finely chop, then allow to soak 5 minutes in lime juice. Add other ingredients and blend well. Fold in chilled gelatin. Decorate with thin slices of unpeeled cucumbers, if desired.

Yield: 6-8 servings.

ASPARAGUS PANZANELLA

1 large round loaf country-style bread, cut into 1-inch cubes, about 4 cups
2 pounds asparagus
1 seedless cucumber, peeled and cut into ½-inch wedges
16 ounce container cherry tomatoes cut in half
5 plum tomatoes, seeded and cut in wedges
1 bell pepper, seeded and chopped (½ yellow, ½ orange)
1 small red onion, thinly sliced
¾ cup kalamata olives, pitted
¼ cup capers, drained
1 shallot, finely chopped
1 clove garlic, mashed to a paste
2 teaspoons grated lemon rind
¼ cup balsamic vinegar
Salt and freshly ground pepper
½ cup extra virgin olive oil
12 fresh basil leaves, shredded

Spread bread cubes out, uncovered, to dry for 24 hours, or bake in a 300 degree oven for 10-20 minutes, until dried out but not toasted.

Snap off and discard the tough ends of asparagus. Prepare an ice bath. In a medium saucepan, bring salted water to a boil and cook asparagus until bright green and just tender, 2-3 minutes. Transfer to ice bath, then drain.

In a large bowl, combine asparagus, cucumber, tomatoes, bell pepper, onion, olives, and capers.

In a small bowl, whisk together shallots, garlic, lemon rind, and balsamic vinegar. Season with salt and pepper. Add olive oil in a stream, whisking constantly. Pour over asparagus mixture and toss until well coated.

Thirty minutes before serving, add basil and bread cubes. Toss and let stand at room temperature.

Yield 12 servings.

ASPARAGUS

Thickness is a matter of taste. Choose bunches with tightly closed tips without flowering. Stalks should be bright green and firm. Avoid those with stalks that are flattened or wrinkled and feel hollow.

BELL PEPPERS

Select peppers that are very firm all over with taut skin. Flesh should be thick without soft spots or wrinkles. Look for bright green stems. Chiles: Any color you choose should be vibrant and wrinkle free.

HE WHO works his land will have abundant food, but he who chases fantasies lacks judgment. *Proverbs 12:11*

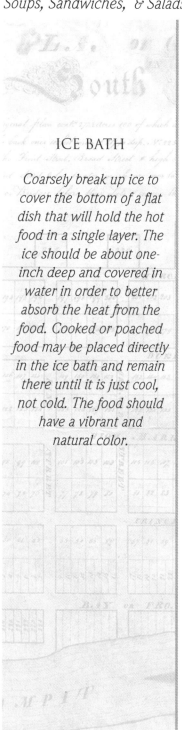

ICE BATH

Coarsely break up ice to cover the bottom of a flat dish that will hold the hot food in a single layer. The ice should be about one-inch deep and covered in water in order to better absorb the heat from the food. Cooked or poached food may be placed directly in the ice bath and remain there until it is just cool, not cold. The food should have a vibrant and natural color.

ORIENTAL SALAD

1	medium/large Napa cabbage	½	cup sesame seeds
1	large bunch fresh spinach	2	(3 ounce) packages ramen noodles, crushed (omit flavor packet)
1	bunch green onions (about 10 onions)	4	tablespoons butter
½	cup slivered almonds		

DRESSING

¼	cup balsamic or red wine vinegar	⅛	cup soy sauce
½	cup light olive oil	¼	cup sugar

Clean cabbage and spinach. Slice cabbage fine, tear spinach, and slice green onions thinly. Mix these together in a large bowl. Brown almonds, sesame seeds, and crushed ramen noodles in butter, being careful not to burn. Then allow to cool. When ready to serve, add to cabbage mixture. Combine dressing ingredients and toss well.

Yield: 8 servings.

MARINATED BROCCOLI SALAD

1	bunch fresh broccoli	4	tablespoons red wine vinegar
1	medium purple onion		
1	cup grated sharp Cheddar cheese	½	cup sugar
8	slices bacon, cooked and crumbled	4	tablespoons mayonnaise

Chop broccoli and onion. Combine with cheese and bacon. Place in airtight container. Bring vinegar, sugar, and mayonnaise to a boil. Pour over broccoli-cheese mixture. Stir to coat broccoli pieces. Cover tightly. Refrigerate overnight. Stir before serving.

Yield: 4-6 servings.

HOLIDAY OR ANY DAY BROCCOLI SALAD

2	large bunches fresh broccoli (2½-3 pounds)	1	(6 ounce) package dried apricots, diced
2	cups mayonnaise	1	(8 ounce) block extra sharp Cheddar cheese, shredded
½	cup sugar		
½	cup red wine vinegar		
½	teaspoon salt	2	(2.25 ounce) packages slivered almonds, toasted
¾	teaspoon freshly ground pepper		
		1	small purple onion, diced
2	(6 ounce) packages sweetened dried cranberries		

Cut florets from broccoli. Chop florets and set aside. Cut broccoli stalks into 1-inch pieces. Pulse in a food processor 6-8 times or until finely chopped. Whisk together mayonnaise, sugar, vinegar, salt, and pepper in a large bowl. Add florets, chopped stalk, cranberries, and remaining ingredients. Toss to coat. Serve immediately or chill up to 6 hours.

Yield: 18-20 servings.

Ocean Spray Craisins were recommended for this recipe.

CLASSIC STUFFED EGGS
HARBOR HOUSE BED AND BREAKFAST

15	large eggs, hard-cooked	1	teaspoon Worcestershire sauce
3	tablespoons mayonnaise		
1	tablespoon sugar	⅛	teaspoon salt
1	tablespoon Dijon mustard		Paprika
1	tablespoon vinegar		Garnish: fresh herb sprigs
1	teaspoon hot sauce		

Peel and cut eggs lengthwise. Carefully remove yolks and mash with a fork. Blend in next 8 ingredients. Spoon into egg white halves. Garnish with fresh herb sprigs, if desired.

Yield: 30 stuffed eggs.

HOW TO HARD-COOK EGGS

Place eggs in a single layer in a saucepan. Be sure the eggs are covered with cold water. Bring to a boil; cover, remove from heat and let stand 15 minutes. Drain and fill the pan with cold water and ice. Cover the pot and shake so the eggs crack all over. Peel under cold running water, starting at the larger end.

BOK CHOY SALAD

2 (3 ounce) packages Ramen
noodles
1/2 cup sunflower seeds
3 tablespoons slivered
almonds, chopped
1/2 cup sugar
1/4 cup olive oil
1/4 cup cider vinegar
2 tablespoons soy sauce
1 bok choy, shredded
6 green onions, chopped

Preheat oven to 350°.
Remove flavor packets from
Ramen noodles; reserve for
another use. Crumble noodles.
Combine noodles, sunflower
seeds, and almonds. Spread
on 15x10-inch jelly roll pan.
Bake for 8-10 minutes or until
golden brown; set aside. Bring
sugar, oil, vinegar, and soy
sauce to a boil in a saucepan
over medium heat. Remove
from heat; cool. Place bok
choy and green onions in a
large bowl. Drizzle with sugar
mixture. Add Ramen-noodle
mixture tossing well.
Serve immediately.

Yield: 6-8 servings.

CHIVE DEVILED EGGS

1	dozen large eggs, hard-cooked	½	teaspoon salt
½	cup mayonnaise	½	teaspoon dry mustard
1	tablespoon lemon juice		Garnishes: chopped fresh chives, fresh flat-leaf parsley sprigs
⅛	teaspoon hot sauce		
2	tablespoons finely chopped fresh chives		

Peel and cut eggs in half lengthwise. Carefully remove yolks. Mash egg yolks. Stir in mayonnaise, lemon juice, hot sauce, and next 3 ingredients. Spoon or pipe egg yolk mixture evenly into egg white halves. Cover and chill at least 1 hour or until ready to serve. Garnish, if desired.

To pipe the yolk mixture into egg white halves for a fancier look, fill a plastic bag with the yolk mixture, cut a hole in one corner, and press the bag to squeeze the yolk mixture into the halves.

Yield: 2 dozen.

SPINACH STRAWBERRY SALAD

DRESSING

½	cup vegetable oil	1½	tablespoons grated onion
½	cup sugar	2	tablespoons poppy seeds
¼	cup cider vinegar	¼	teaspoon paprika
1½	teaspoons Worcestershire sauce		

SALAD
1   bag fresh ready-to-serve
    spinach

TOPPING

1	pint fresh strawberries, sliced	½	cup slivered almonds, toasted if desired

Mix dressing ingredients. Place spinach in bowl. Toss with dressing. Top with strawberries and almonds. Serve immediately.

Yield: 6 servings.

Remaining dressing keeps well in the refrigerator.

SPINACH AND CRANBERRY SALAD WITH WARM CHUTNEY DRESSING

1	cup toasted pecans	¾	cup dried cranberries
2	(6 ounce) packages baby spinach	4	ounces Blue cheese Warm Chutney Dressing
6	bacon slices, cooked and crumbled		

Toss all of the above ingredients while the dressing is still warm. Serve immediately.

WARM CHUTNEY DRESSING

6	tablespoons balsamic vinegar	2	tablespoons honey
⅓	cup bottled mango chutney	2	garlic cloves, minced
2	tablespoons Dijon mustard	¼	cup olive oil

Cook the first 5 ingredients in a saucepan over medium heat, stirring constantly for 3 minutes. Stir in olive oil, blending well; cook 1 minute.

Yield: 1 cup.

CORNBREAD SALAD

CORNBREAD
2 (8 ½ ounce) boxes cornbread mix

Bake according to package directions. Cube or crumble cornbread and set aside.

SALAD

1	pound bacon fried, crispy and crumbled	1	cup diced onions
3	cups diced tomatoes	¼	cup sweet pickle relish
1	cup diced bell peppers	¼	cup sweet pickle juice
		1	cup mayonnaise

Discard bacon grease. Mix bacon, vegetables, pickle relish, pickle juice, and mayonnaise. Add to cornbread and mix well. Refrigerate until ready to serve.

Yield: 6-8 servings.

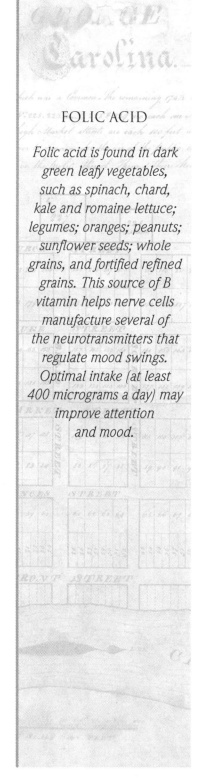

FOLIC ACID

Folic acid is found in dark green leafy vegetables, such as spinach, chard, kale and romaine lettuce; legumes; oranges; peanuts; sunflower seeds; whole grains, and fortified refined grains. This source of B vitamin helps nerve cells manufacture several of the neurotransmitters that regulate mood swings. Optimal intake (at least 400 micrograms a day) may improve attention and mood.

CLASSIC PASTA SALAD

1   pound rotini pasta
2   tablespoons fresh chopped, or 1 tablespoon dried dill weed
1   (1 ounce) package Ranch salad dressing mix
    Juice of ½ lemon
2   tablespoons buttermilk

½   cup mayonnaise
½   cup sour cream
    Salt and pepper to taste
4   stalks celery, finely chopped
1   red onion, finely chopped
1   cup frozen green peas, thawed

Cook pasta in boiling water until tender. Drain and rinse with cold water. In a large mixing bowl: combine the dill, Ranch salad dressing mix, lemon juice, buttermilk, mayonnaise, and sour cream. Stir to combine thoroughly. Season with salt and pepper. Gently stir the dressing into the vegetables and cooked pasta. Chill for at least 2 hours or until serving time.

Yield: 4-6 servings.

TABOOLI

½   cup cracked wheat, finely ground
1   large bunch fresh flat leafed parsley, finely chopped
1   bunch green onions, thinly sliced, including part of green
2   medium size tomatoes, finely diced

1   large cucumber, peeled, seeded, and finely diced
10-12 fresh mint leaves, chopped OR 1 teaspoon dried mint leaves
¼   cup lemon juice
¼   cup light olive oil
    Salt and pepper to taste

Put cracked wheat in a small bowl, and add boiling water to cover. Let sit 5 minutes; then drain, squeezing as much water out as possible. Place next 5 ingredients in a large bowl. Add wheat, lemon juice, olive oil, salt, and pepper. Chill in refrigerator for at least one hour. Toss salad again before serving. May be stored in refrigerator, tightly covered, for several days. Taste improves as it marinates.

Tossed Salad with Walnut Toasted Goat Cheese

Goat Cheese Slices

⅓	cup fresh soft breadcrumbs	1	(5½ ounce) log mild goat cheese	
⅓	cup ground walnuts			
		1½	tablespoons walnut oil	

Combine breadcrumbs and ground walnuts in a low-sided dish. Cut the cheese into 6 even slices. Dip each slice in walnut oil and then into the crumb/nut mixture. Press crumbs onto all surfaces of each cheese slice, put in 1 layer on a plate and refrigerate 15-30 minutes.

Yield: 1 cup.

Mixed Greens

Mixed greens of any kind for 6 people — a 9-ounce bag is good.

Wash and dry greens. Place in large bowl.

Dressing

1	tablespoon Dijon mustard	½	cup olive oil	
½	teaspoon sugar	4	tablespoons red wine vinegar	
¼	teaspoon salt			
¼	teaspoon fresh pepper		Minced parsley or tarragon	

Combine dressing ingredients in a covered glass jar and shake well. Chill until 10 minutes before serving.

Preheat oven to 350°. Place cheese slices on a sprayed cookie sheet and bake for only 4-5 minutes. (If heated too long, they lose their shape.) Toss greens with dressing in a bowl. Put a portion of greens on each serving plate with a slice of baked cheese on top. Serve immediately.

Yield: 6 servings.

Dried cranberries or toasted or candied nuts may be added for variety.

It sounds harder than it is as all can be done in advance except assembling and baking the cheese at the last minute.

Give us grateful hearts, our Father, for all thy mercies, and make us mindful of the needs of others, through Jesus Christ our Lord, Amen.

Book of Common Prayer

CAULIFLOWER SALAD

1 head cauliflower
(cut into small pieces)
1 (10 ounce) box frozen peas
½ cup mayonnaise
Juice of 1 lemon
1 teaspoon dill weed
¼ cup minced red onion
1 (8 ounce) can sliced water
chestnuts, drained
½ cup cashews

Mix together all ingredients
except cashews. Chill for
2 hours. Add cashews
immediately before serving.

Yield: 6-8 servings.

GREEN SALAD WITH MANDARIN ORANGES

DRESSING

½	cup tarragon vinegar	½	cup sugar
½	cup salad oil	1	teaspoon salt
½	tablespoon Worcestershire sauce		Pepper to taste
1	teaspoon dry mustard	2	teaspoons minced parsley
		1	medium onion, thinly sliced

Mix all ingredients, making sure sugar is dissolved before adding onions. Refrigerate several hours.

SALAD

	Mixture of salad greens (1 head green or red leaf lettuce and 1 package spring mix, to desired amount)	2	(11 ounce) cans Mandarin oranges, drained
		½	cup toasted, slivered almonds

Just before serving, pour dressing over salad. Toss oranges and almonds with greens. Serve immediately.

Yield: 8-10 servings.

HAM AND BLUE CHEESE PASTA SALAD

3	cups dried bow tie pasta	½	teaspoon freshly ground pepper
1	cup coarsely chopped pecans, toasted	1	(4 ounce) package cooked ham, cut into thin strips
⅓	cup grated Parmesan cheese	1	(4 ounce) package blue cheese, crumbled
2	tablespoons chopped fresh parsley	1	garlic clove, minced
1	tablespoon fresh rosemary	¼	cup olive oil

Cook pasta, according to directions on package, and drain well. Place in a large serving bowl. Add pecans and next 7 ingredients, tossing gently to combine. Add oil, stirring gently to coat mixture. Serve immediately or cover and chill thoroughly, if desired.

RASPBERRY-TOMATO ASPIC

1⅔	cups tomato juice	⅛	teaspoon crushed dried rosemary
2	tablespoons sugar		
2	tablespoons finely chopped fresh mint	1	(¼ ounce) envelope unflavored gelatin
2	tablespoons red wine vinegar	½	cup cold water
2	tablespoons fresh lemon juice	1	(3 ounce) package raspberry gelatin
½	bay leaf		Garnishes: fresh mint sprigs, lemon slices
			Chicken or shrimp salad

Bring tomato juice and next 6 ingredients to a boil in a large saucepan; reduce heat, and simmer 5 minutes. Pour tomato juice mixture through a wire-mesh strainer into a large mixing bowl, discarding solids. Sprinkle unflavored gelatin over cold water; let stand 1 minute. Stir softened gelatin mixture into tomato juice mixture, stirring until gelatin dissolves. Prepare raspberry gelatin according to package directions; do not chill. Add to tomato juice mixture, stirring until combined. Pour mixture into 10 (6 ounce) punch cups; chill 8 hours or until firm. Garnish, if desired. Serve with chicken or shrimp salad.

Yield: 10 servings.

MOTHER'S TOMATO ASPIC

1	(46 ounce) can tomato-vegetable juice, divided use	2	teaspoons lemon juice
			Hot sauce, to taste
			Vegetable cooking spray
3	bay leaves	3-4	stalks celery, finely chopped
3	(¼ ounce) envelopes unflavored gelatin	1	(13 ounce) jar green olives
	Worcestershire sauce, to taste		

Heat 2 cups of tomato-vegetable juice with bay leaves to boiling point. Mix together another cup of juice and 3 envelopes of gelatin. Add this to hot mixture, boil, and remove bay leaves. Add Worcestershire sauce, lemon juice, and hot sauce. Add another cup of the tomato-vegetable juice, stir and cool slightly. Spray salad mold with vegetable spray and place olives and celery on bottom. Pour the liquid into mold and chill.

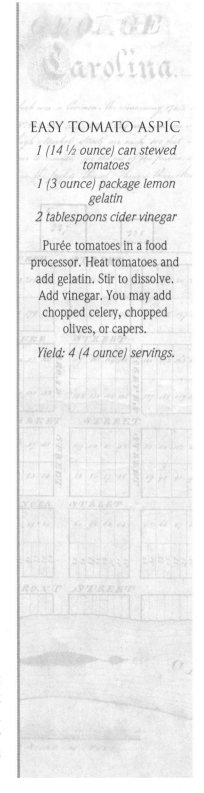

EASY TOMATO ASPIC

1 (14 ½ ounce) can stewed tomatoes

1 (3 ounce) package lemon gelatin

2 tablespoons cider vinegar

Purée tomatoes in a food processor. Heat tomatoes and add gelatin. Stir to dissolve. Add vinegar. You may add chopped celery, chopped olives, or capers.

Yield: 4 (4 ounce) servings.

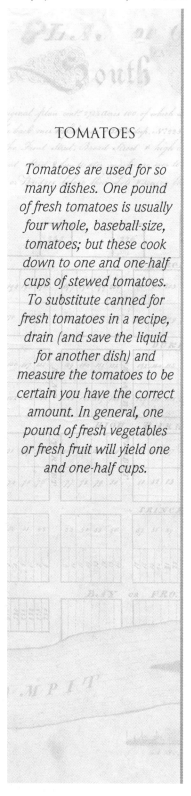

TACO SALAD

1	pound lean ground beef	2	large tomatoes, seeded and chopped
1	(1¼ ounce) package taco seasoning mix	1	pound sharp Cheddar cheese, grated
1	(15½ ounce) can kidney beans, drained	1	(16 ounce) chilled bottle tomato based salad dressing
1	head iceberg lettuce, torn in pieces	1	(9 ounce) package plain large tortilla chips, crushed
2	medium onions, chopped		
1	large green bell pepper, chopped		

Prepare ground beef and taco seasoning according to package directions. Set aside to cool. Drain the beans thoroughly. In a very large mixing bowl, tear up lettuce. Chop onions, bell pepper, and tomatoes. Add to the lettuce: beans, grated cheese, and seasoned ground beef. Toss. Add half to all of the bottle of tomato-based dressing, according to your taste. Toss. Add crushed tortilla chips to taste. Toss again. Serve in very large pasta/salad bowl.

Yield: 12 servings.

Catalina salad dressing was recommended for this recipe.

Because ingredient preparation is time consuming, make this the night before. Put the onions, beans, peppers, tomatoes, cheese, and beef in small zip lock bags on top of the torn up lettuce. Microwave the beef to room temperature before adding to the salad, and toss the ingredients. It does the job more thoroughly and is gentler on the chips.

BLUE CHEESE SLAW

1	head cabbage, shredded	½	cup sour cream
4	green onions, chopped	2	tablespoons lemon juice
1	cup mayonnaise		Salt and pepper
1	tablespoon horseradish	1	sweet red pepper, cut into strips
4	ounces blue cheese		

Combine all ingredients. Cover and chill several hours or overnight.

WARM POTATO SALAD NIÇOISE

DRESSING

3 tablespoons white wine vinegar
2 tablespoons water
1 tablespoon Dijon mustard

1 tablespoon anchovy paste, optional
3 tablespoons light olive oil
2 cloves garlic, minced

Combine vinegar and water. Whisk in mustard and anchovy paste. Add oil, whisking until smooth. Whisk in garlic.

POTATOES AND VEGETABLES

2 pounds red potatoes, cut into chunks
½ pound fresh green beans, halved
4 green onions, chopped

2 stalks celery, chopped
¼ cup freshly minced parsley
1 (6½ ounce) can white tuna, drained

Cook potatoes in boiling water to cover until barely tender. Add beans and cook a few more minutes until beans are just tender. Drain and toss with ¼ cup dressing while still hot. Let cool until mixture is slightly warm. Add remaining ingredients and additional dressing to taste.

Yield: 4 servings.

WILD-RICE SHRIMP SALAD

1 (16 ounce) package long grain & wild rice
1 (7 ounce) jar marinated artichoke quarters
1½ pounds shrimp; cooked, peeled, and deveined
4 green onions, sliced

¼ cup chopped yellow bell pepper
¼ cup chopped red or green bell pepper
12 black olives, sliced
⅓ cup mayonnaise
¼ teaspoon curry powder

Cook rice according to package directions and cool. Drain artichokes, reserving 3 tablespoons liquid.

Combine shrimp, rice, artichokes, onions, peppers, and olives in a large bowl. Set the bowl aside. In a separate bowl combine reserved artichoke liquid, mayonnaise, and curry powder. Pour over shrimp mixture and toss.

Cover and chill 5 hours. Serve on a bed of baby greens.

Yield: 8 servings.

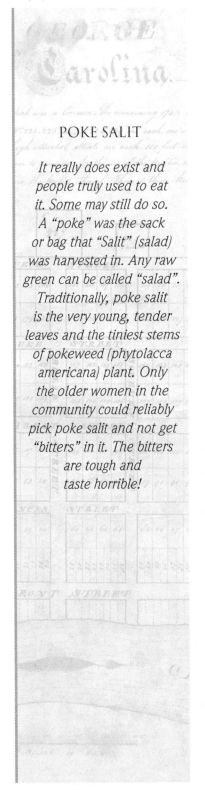

POKE SALIT

It really does exist and people truly used to eat it. Some may still do so. A "poke" was the sack or bag that "Salit" (salad) was harvested in. Any raw green can be called "salad". Traditionally, poke salit is the very young, tender leaves and the tiniest stems of pokeweed (phytolacca americana) plant. Only the older women in the community could reliably pick poke salit and not get "bitters" in it. The bitters are tough and taste horrible!

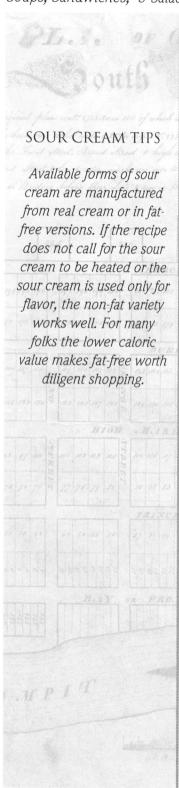

ARTICHOKE-SHRIMP PASTA SALAD

PASTA

1 (9 ounce) can marinated artichoke hearts, quartered and drained

1 pound shrimp, cooked, peeled, and deveined

1 (8 ounce) package bow tie pasta, cooked, drained, and cooled

Combine these ingredients in a large bowl.

DRESSING

¼ cup red wine vinegar

2 tablespoons Dijon

1 tablespoon tarragon

1 egg yolk

1 tablespoon minced shallots

½ cup olive oil

2 tablespoons vegetable oil

Salt and pepper to taste

Combine vinegar, mustard, tarragon, egg yolk, and shallots in a food processor. Blend well. Gradually add the olive oil and vegetable oil while the machine is running. Season with salt and pepper.

Pour dressing over pasta and stir gently. You may need to add more salt and pepper. Refrigerate at least 3 hours.

This salad is also great with added chicken.

BLUE CHEESE SALAD DRESSING

1 cup mayonnaise

1 cup sour cream

4 ounces blue cheese

¼ teaspoon salt

1 tablespoon Worcestershire sauce

1 teaspoon lemon juice

Mix all ingredients. Chill. Serve over lettuce.

May garnish with ½ cup parmesan cheese and crumbled bacon, if desired.

ARTICHOKE RICE SALAD

1   (10 ounce) package
      chicken flavored rice
2   green onions, minced
1   green pepper, minced
½   cup chopped green olives
½   teaspoon curry

½   cup mayonnaise
2   (6 ounce) jars marinated
      artichoke hearts
3   chicken breasts, cooked
      and chopped OR
      2 (6 ounce) cans white
      chicken meat

Cook rice according to package directions, omitting butter. Cool in large bowl. Add onions, pepper, and olives. In separate bowl, combine curry powder, mayonnaise, and juice from 1 jar of artichokes. Mix and add to rice. Drain and chop remaining artichoke hearts. Add artichokes and chicken. Toss all together.

GERMAN STYLE SLAW

1   (1½-2 pounds) head
      cabbage shredded
1   medium onion, chopped or
      shredded

½   green or red bell pepper,
      diced
¾   cup sugar

Combine cabbage, onion, and bell pepper in large glass bowl. Add sugar. Mix well. Cover and refrigerate overnight.

DRESSING (MARINADE)

1   cup apple cider vinegar
½   cup olive oil (may
      substitute canola)
¼   cup sugar

1   teaspoon salt
1   teaspoon celery seed
1   teaspoon dry mustard

NEXT DAY: Combine in sauce pan all marinade ingredients. Bring dressing to boil, reduce heat and simmer about 3 minutes. Let stand several minutes to slightly cool. Drain most of the juice from the cabbage mix. Add the heated dressing and mix well. Cover and refrigerate several hours (or preferably overnight).

Slaw will stay crisp more than 1 week.

QUEEN ANNE'S BROCCOLI SLAW

1 (8 ounce) bag broccoli slaw

1 (4 ounce) bag dried
cranberries

3 ounces dried feta cheese

¼ cup scallions, finely
chopped

¼ cup toasted almonds
chopped

Mix all ingredients together. Toss with dressing when ready to serve.

Dressing

¼ cup salad oil

3 tablespoons plus
1 teaspoon sugar

2 tablespoons
red wine vinegar

2 tablespoons soy sauce

⅛ teaspoon pepper

Heat slightly to dissolve sugar.

SWEET POTATO SALAD

2	pounds sweet potatoes	4	hard-cooked eggs, chopped
1½	cups mayonnaise		
2	teaspoons Dijon mustard	1½	cups finely chopped celery
¼	teaspoon salt	8	green onions, sliced

Place sweet potatoes in a large saucepan and cover with water. Cover and boil gently until the potatoes can easily be pierced with the tip of a sharp knife, about 30-45 minutes. Drain. When potatoes are cool, peel, and dice. In a large bowl, combine mayonnaise, mustard, and salt. Stir in eggs, celery, and onions. Add potatoes; stir gently to mix. Cover and refrigerate for 2-4 hours.

Yield: 8-10 servings.

GINNY'S COLE SLAW DRESSING

⅓	cup mayonnaise	½	teaspoon salt
1	tablespoon vinegar	1½	teaspoons celery seed
1	tablespoon sugar		

Combine all ingredients, and stir into chopped cabbage. Chill.

Yield: ½ cup.

RANCH-STYLE BUTTERMILK DRESSING

⅔	cup 1% buttermilk	2	tablespoons minced fresh parsley
⅓	cup reduced-fat mayonnaise		
¼	cup reduced-fat sour cream	1	garlic clove, minced
		1	teaspoon dill weed

Whisk together and chill.

MONTICELLO FRENCH DRESSING

1	cup salad oil	½	cup sugar
⅓	cup vinegar	⅓	cup catsup
	Juice of ½ lemon	1	teaspoon salt
1	teaspoon paprika	½	teaspoon grated onion

Mix ingredients and shake well in a pint jar. Keep it refrigerated.

Yield: 2 cups.

MRS. LOUIS OVERTON

GRAY'S DRESSING FOR FRUIT SALADS

12	marshmallows	1	(8 ounce) carton sour cream
2	tablespoons water		Juice of 1 orange
1	(8 ounce) package cream cheese		

Melt marshmallows in water in top of double boiler. Add cream cheese, sour cream, and orange juice. Stir until blended.

MARGARET RICHARDSON

TOMATO FRENCH DRESSING

1	(10¾ ounce) can tomato soup	½	teaspoon red pepper
¾	cup vinegar	1	teaspoon grated onion
½	teaspoon paprika	1	teaspoon dry mustard
½	teaspoon Worcestershire sauce	1½	cups salad oil

Combine in quart jar and chill. Shake well before using.

Yield: 1 quart.

ELIZABETH FORD

COTTAGE CHEESE

Cottage cheese takes its name literally from the cottages where it was made by farmers' wives long ago. Whey and other milk solids were hung in cheese cloth bags in a spot outdoors until the cheese had lost enough moisture and gained the consistency the maker wanted. Creamed cottage cheese was allowed to hang for less time and had varying amounts of the remaining liquids stirred into the finished product. Uncreamed cottage cheese was drier though still soft. Both varieties are produced under carefully regulated standards today.

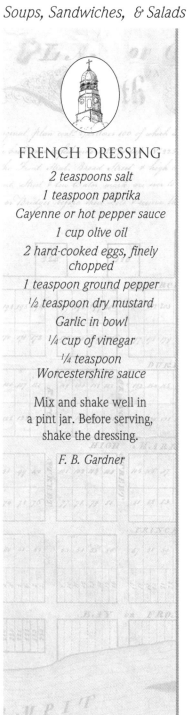

FRENCH DRESSING

2 teaspoons salt

1 teaspoon paprika

Cayenne or hot pepper sauce

1 cup olive oil

2 hard-cooked eggs, finely chopped

1 teaspoon ground pepper

½ teaspoon dry mustard

Garlic in bowl

¼ cup of vinegar

¼ teaspoon Worcestershire sauce

Mix and shake well in a pint jar. Before serving, shake the dressing.

F. B. Gardner

SALAD DRESSING FOR LETTUCE

2   tablespoons Dijon mustard

2   cloves garlic, crushed or minced

¼   cup tarragon vinegar

¾   cup olive oil

Salt and freshly ground pepper to taste

Whisk mustard, garlic, and vinegar together. Add olive oil slowly while whisking. Add salt and freshly ground pepper. Pour into salad dressing jar. Keep it refrigerated.

Yield: 1 cup.

FOR I *was hungry and you gave me something to eat, I was thirsty and you gave me something to drink, I was a stranger and you invited me in. Matthew 25:35*

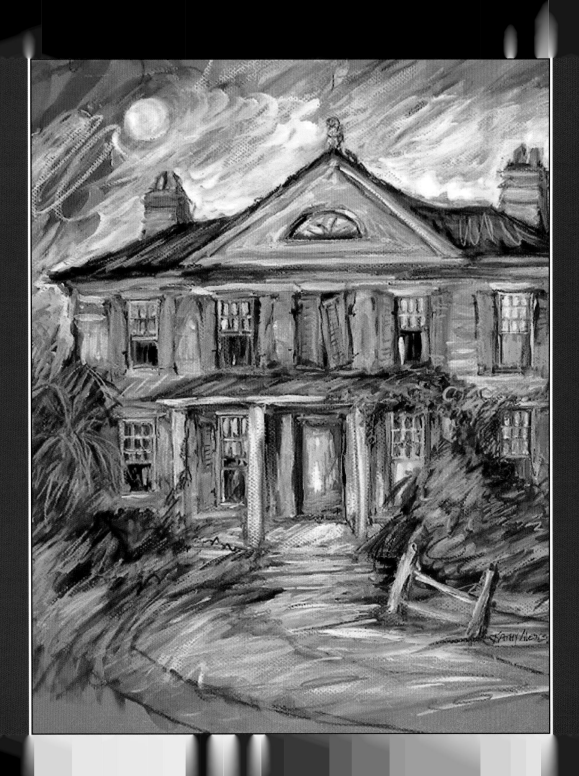

Friendfield Plantation

Artist: Kathy Metts

Friendfield Plantation, originally known as Washington after the President, is located on the Sampit River. It was not until 1818 that the name was changed to Friendfield, commemorating an instance of brotherly love. When Francis Withers bought the plantation, he lacked funds to complete the transaction, so he borrowed from his brother, James. When he attempted to repay the loan, his brother refused to accept the money and tore up the note. This act prompted Francis to rename the plantation Friendfield. The plantation passed into the hands of Withers' stepdaughter, Elizabeth Warham, who had married Dr. Alexius Mador Forster. Dr. and Mrs. Forster made their home there. During the Civil War, Dr. Forster served as a surgeon with Marion's Men of Winyah (named for Francis Marion, the Swamp Fox, of Revolutionary fame). The plantation was finally sold as a hunting club. In 1926, the house was destroyed by fire leaving only the raised brick basement.

The late Mr. And Mrs. Radcliffe Cheston of Philadelphia built the present mansion house in 1931 as a winter home. The house is built on the original site using the old porch and some of the old foundations and chimneys. Mr. and Mrs. Cheston restored the gardens so that Friendfield has once again come into its own as a place of beauty and charm. Friendfield is now owned by Daniel K. Thorne and Frances Cheston Train.

This property is on the National Register of Historic Places.

PAULINE'S CRAB CAKES
PAULINE GRATE (COOK AT FRIENDFIELD PLANTATION)

1	pound crabmeat	2	heaping tablespoons flour
1	large onion	3	eggs
	Salt and pepper to taste		Solid vegetable shortening
1	tablespoon Worcestershire sauce		

Pick through crabmeat to remove bits of shell. Keep refrigerated until ready to combine with other ingredients. Chop the onion very finely. Combine crabmeat, onion, salt, pepper, and Worcestershire sauce. Sprinkle the flour into the mixture and combine thoroughly. Separate 2 eggs. Combine 2 yolks with the remaining whole egg and beat until blended. Combine with crab mixture. Beat 1 egg white until stiff; gently fold into crabmeat mixture. Discard the remaining egg white. Melt shortening in a cast iron skillet to a depth of 1 inch. When shortening is hot, drop in crab mixture by large spoonfuls. Cook until lightly browned, approximately 2 minutes on each side.

Crisco Vegetable Shortening was recommended for this recipe.

LOBSTER AND JUMBO LUMP CRAB CAKE
FRANK'S RESTAURANT, PAWLEYS ISLAND, SC

½	pound jumbo lump crab	1	tablespoon Dijon mustard
½	pound lobster claw and knuckle meat	½	teaspoon celery salt
1	egg	1	cup panko (Japanese) breadcrumbs, divided
¼	cup mayonnaise		Olive oil

Preheat oven to 400°. Pick through crab to remove any shells, leaving large lumps intact. Place crab in a bowl with the lobster meat. In a separate bowl, mix together egg, mayonnaise, mustard, and celery salt. Add to lobster mixture and toss well, trying not to break up crabmeat. Sprinkle ¼ cup panko over mixture and mix well. Refrigerate for 15 minutes. Form into 4-ounce cakes and roll in remaining panko until well coated. Refrigerate until ready to cook. Heat olive oil in sauté pan. Over medium heat, brown cakes on one side, approximately 2 minutes. Flip cakes and place in oven for approximately 5 minutes or until heated through.

Yield: 12 cakes.

CRABBY FACTS

Blue/Soft Shell Crab

Flavor and Texture: When mild-tasting blue crabs shed their hard shells, they're known as soft-shell crabs. At that point, they're eaten whole and have a sweet flavor and crisp texture. Peak season: May through August. Best served: In crab cakes and salads. Soft shells are best sautéed or deep fried, and put in sandwiches or sushi rolls.

Stone Crab

Flavor and Texture: These are sweet and dense, and have a more leathery taste than other varieties. Peak Season: Available year-round. Best served: Split and dipped in butter or a spicy cocktail sauce.

Snow Crab

Flavor and Texture: This variety has finer, lighter, sweeter meat than others. Peak Season: Available year-round. Best Served: In crab dips or stuffing for prawns or sole.

DEVILED CRAB

*1½ cups coarsely
crushed saltines*

½ cup melted butter

1 egg

2 tablespoons mayonnaise

1 teaspoon yellow mustard

*¼ teaspoon
Worcestershire sauce*

1-2 drops hot sauce

¼ teaspoon black pepper

1 pound lump crabmeat

Preheat oven to 350°.
Combine saltines and butter.
Set aside. In a large bowl,
add egg and beat slightly;
add mayonnaise, mustard,
Worcestershire sauce, hot
sauce, and black pepper.
Add ½ of crumb mixture.
Check crab for shells, being
careful not to break up lumps.
Gently fold in crab. Lightly fill
individual shells or a casserole
dish. Do not pack down. Cover
with remaining crumbs. Bake
until light brown and bubbly,
about 15-30 minutes.

Yield: 4 servings.

**Hellmann's mayonnaise was
recommended for this recipe.**

Mary Loyal Collins

CLAMS WALLACE

1	medium onion	6	strips of bacon
½	teaspoon tarragon	½	teaspoon dried tarragon
½	cup dry vermouth		Pepper
2	dozen small clams		

Mince onion. Combine with tarragon and vermouth. Let stand at least
1 hour. Open clams; save larger shells. Cut bacon in 2-inch pieces. Place
one clam in each shell. Cover with a spoonful of vermouth mixture. Place
a piece of bacon on top. Broil about 6 inches from heat until bacon is done.
Serve at once.

Yield: 6 servings.

*Freeze clams in shells. Put clams in sink or large pot and cover with hot water for
a few minutes. Shells will pop open and clams are easily removed.*

CLAM FRITTERS

	Clams, steamed to open		Flour, seasoned with
	Evaporated milk		seafood seasoning
		1	cup vegetable oil

Remove clams from shells and set aside. Dip in evaporated milk and dredge
in flour. Fry in oil. Drain.

Adjust ingredients according to the quantity of clams you have.

Serve with aïolo sauce for grown ups or ketchup for kids.

AÏOLO SAUCE

2	egg yolks	1	cup olive oil
2	garlic cloves, minced	1	teaspoon fresh lemon juice
½	teaspoon salt	½	teaspoon water
½	teaspoon pepper		

Whisk together egg yolks, garlic, salt, and pepper. Slowly add oil; whisk.
Slowly add lemon juice and water while whisking. Chill.

Yield: 1½ cups.

DEVILED CRAB

1	sleeve saltine crackers		Juice of one lemon
1	pound crabmeat	¼	teaspoon Worcestershire sauce
2	tablespoons mayonnaise		Salt to taste
½	cup melted butter	¼	cup milk
½	teaspoon dry mustard		Paprika
¼	teaspoon mace		

Preheat oven to 325°. Crush crackers, reserving some for topping. Mix all ingredients together. Stuff crab shells or ramekins. Sprinkle tops with cracker crumbs and paprika. Bake for 20 minutes.

Yield: 5 servings.

CRAB QUICHE

½	cup mayonnaise	4	ounces Swiss cheese, grated
2	tablespoons flour	⅓	cup grated onion
2	eggs, beaten		Large mushroom slices for garnish
½	cup milk	1	deep-dish pie shell, unbaked
1	(7½ ounce) can crabmeat OR ½ pound fresh crabmeat		

Preheat oven to 350°. Blend first 4 ingredients. Add crabmeat, cheese, and onion. Pour into uncooked deep-dish pie shell. Decorate top with slices of large mushrooms. Place pie pan on cookie sheet. Bake 40-45 minutes.

Yield: 6-8 servings.

Prepared filling may be mixed ahead and kept refrigerated until ready to bake. Do not fill pie crust until ready to bake.

NOTES

CRAB CAKES

ROZ'S RICE MILL CAFE, PAWLEYS ISLAND, SC

1	pound lump crabmeat, free of shells	½	green bell pepper, minced
1	egg white		Mayonnaise, enough to bind together, added a little at a time
¼	teaspoon celery seed		
½	teaspoon seafood seasoning		Panko breadcrumbs
2	stalks celery, minced		Canola oil

Combine all ingredients, except breadcrumbs and oil. Try not to overwork, keeping crabmeat in lump texture. Roll cakes in panko crumbs to coat. Fry in canola oil at medium-high heat until brown on both sides, 2-3 minutes.

Yield: 4-6 crab cakes.

Panko breadcrumbs are found in specialty stores.

CRAB CASSEROLE

¼	cup butter	1	egg, beaten
¼	onion, finely chopped		Salt and pepper to taste
12	saltine crackers, crumbled	3	tablespoons mustard and mayonnaise sauce
1	pound white crabmeat, free of shells	1	tablespoon lemon juice
3	tablespoons sherry wine (not cooking sherry)	2	teaspoons Worcestershire sauce

Preheat oven to 350°. Lightly sauté onion in butter. In a large bowl, mix cracker crumbs with onion and mix lightly. Add crabmeat and all other ingredients and mix lightly. Pour ingredients into a 12x8-inch baking dish. Crumble 4 additional crackers and sprinkle on top. Bake uncovered for 30 minutes.

Yield: 8 servings.

This recipe can also be used as a hot crab dip with crackers. If so, add 1 can mushroom soup and 2 tablespoons more sherry.

Yield: 50 servings, as an appetizer.

CLASSIC CRAB SOUFFLÉ

1 (8-ounce) package cream cheese, at room temperature
1 egg, slightly beaten
¾ cup mayonnaise
Juice of 1 lemon

1 tablespoon dried onion OR 2 tablespoons fresh onion, finely chopped
1 (7½ ounce) can crabmeat, rinsed, drained, and checked for shells
Parsley

Preheat oven to 350°. Combine all but the crabmeat and parsley in food processor. Fold in crabmeat. Pour into 2½-quart soufflé dish. Bake for 25 minutes. Garnish with parsley and serve with table crackers.

Yield: 8-10 servings.

SHRIMP AND CRAB TRIUMPH

1 cup mayonnaise
2 tablespoons prepared mustard
1 teaspoon Worcestershire sauce
1 tablespoon parsley flakes
2 teaspoons capers
¼ teaspoon curry powder

¼ teaspoon red pepper
½ cup shredded bread
½ cup sherry
½ cup chopped celery
½ cup chopped onion
1 pound shrimp, peeled
1 pound crabmeat

Preheat oven to 325°. Mix together all ingredients in order given. Place in 1½-quart ovenproof casserole dish. Bake 30-40 minutes.

Yield: 8 servings.

KEEP *falsehood and lies far from me; give me neither poverty nor riches, but give me only my daily bread.*
Proverbs 30:7

QUICK PAN-FRIED FISH FILLETS

¾ cup all-purpose baking mix
½ cup yellow cornmeal
1 tablespoon seafood seasoning
4 (4-6 ounce) catfish fillets
½ cup Ranch dressing
3 tablespoons vegetable oil
Lemon wedges

Combine first 3 ingredients in a shallow bowl. Pat catfish fillets dry with paper towels; brush both sides of each fillet evenly with dressing. Dredge in cornmeal mixture; lightly press cornmeal mixture onto fillets. Cook catfish in hot vegetable oil in a large nonstick skillet over medium-high heat 3-5 minutes on each side or until fish just flakes with a fork. Serve immediately with lemon wedges.

Yield: 4 servings.

Fish generally cooks 10 minutes per inch of thickness. Therefore, thicker catfish will take longer to cook. Lower the temperature slightly.

Bisquick Baking Mix was recommended for this recipe.

BAKED SEAFOOD

1C each *(or each)*

1 large green pepper *(or*
1 small onion
1 cup celery
1 cup cooked crabmeat
1 cup cooked shrimp, peeled
1 cup mayonnaise
½ teaspoon salt
Pepper to taste
1 teaspoon
Worcestershire sauce
½ cup dry breadcrumbs
Paprika
Lemon slices

Preheat oven to 350°. Finely chop green pepper, onion, and celery. Combine crabmeat and shrimp with the vegetables and mayonnaise. Add salt, pepper, and Worcestershire sauce. Put in individual shells or baking dish; cover with crumbs. Bake 30 minutes. Sprinkle top with paprika and serve with sliced lemon.

Mrs. Frank R. Bourne

4 servings

GRILLED FISH FILLETS WITH ASPARAGUS, ARTICHOKES, AND TOMATOES

3 large tomatoes	4 garlic cloves, minced
2 pounds asparagus, trimmed *cut into 3 diagonal pieces - 3" long* *red*	1 large bay leaf
¼ cup olive oil	¼ cup chopped fresh chives OR green onions
2 (9 ounce) packages frozen artichoke hearts, thawed and patted dry *(slice in half)*	¼ cup fresh chopped parsley
2 cups chicken stock or canned low-salt broth	3 tablespoons drained capers
1 cup dry white wine	1 tablespoon grated lemon peel
6 fresh thyme sprigs OR ½ teaspoon dried thyme	8 (6 ounce) fish fillets
	Salt and pepper

Blanch tomatoes in pot of boiling water for 20 seconds. Drain. Peel tomatoes. Cut tomatoes in half; squeeze out seeds. Chop tomatoes; set aside. Cook asparagus in a large pot of boiling, salted water until crisp-tender, about 4 minutes. Drain. Heat oil in heavy large skillet over medium-high heat. Add artichoke hearts and sauté 5 minutes. Add tomatoes, stock, wine, thyme, garlic, and bay leaf; bring to a boil. Reduce heat and simmer until liquid thickens slightly, about 20 minutes. Add chives, parsley, capers, and lemon peel. Season to taste with salt and pepper. Add asparagus and stir to heat thoroughly. Discard bay leaf. Meanwhile, prepare barbecue grill to medium-high heat or preheat broiler. Season fish with salt and pepper. Grill or broil fish fillets until cooked thoroughly, about 5 minutes per side. Using slotted spoon, divide vegetable mixture among 8 plates. Arrange fish atop vegetables in center of plates. Spoon pan juice over fish.

Yield: 8 servings.

Could use other vegetables: yellow squash, broccoli, zucchini, green beans

THE POOR will eat and be satisfied;

those who seek the Lord will praise Him - may your hearts live forever. Psalm 22:26